CORE SKILLS

Grammar Review

ISBN 0-7398-8945-1

Printed in the United States of America.   6 7 8 9   862   11 10 09

Harcourt Achieve
Rigby • Steck-Vaughn

www.HarcourtAchieve.com
1.800.531.5015

Contents

Contents

Introduction

Core Skills: Grammar Review was developed to help your child improve the language skills he or she needs to succeed. The book emphasizes skills in the key areas of

- grammar
- punctuation
- vocabulary

The lessons included in the book provide many opportunities for your child to practice and apply important grammar skills. These skills will help your child excel in all academic areas, increase his or her scores on standardized tests, and have a greater opportunity for success in his or her career.

About the Book

The book is divided into four units:

- Vocabulary
- Sentences
- Grammar and Usage
- Capitalization and Punctuation

Your child can work through each unit of the book, or you can pinpoint areas that need extra practice.

Lessons have specific instructions and examples and are designed for your child to complete independently. Grammar lessons range from using nouns and verbs to constructing better sentences. With this practice, your child will gain extra confidence as he or she works on daily school lessons or standardized tests.

A thorough answer key is also provided to check the quality of answers.

A Step Toward Success

Practice may not always make perfect, but it is certainly a step in the right direction. The activities in *Core Skills: Grammar Review* are an excellent way to ensure greater success for your child.

Check What You Know

A. Write $\underline{S}$ before each pair of synonyms, $\underline{A}$ before each pair of antonyms, and $\underline{H}$ before each pair of homonyms.

_____ **1.** board, bored   _____ **3.** antique, ancient

_____ **2.** tall, short   _____ **4.** massive, huge

B. Write the homograph for the pair of meanings.

_____ **a.** a piece of hair   **b.** to fasten securely

C. Write $\underline{P}$ before each word with a prefix, $\underline{S}$ before each word with a suffix, and $\underline{C}$ before each compound word.

_____ **1.** overcome   _____ **3.** rusty

_____ **2.** misplace   _____ **4.** interested

D. Write the words that make up each contraction.

_____ _____ **1.** they'll   _____ _____ **2.** we've

E. Underline the word in parentheses that has the more positive connotation.

The (crabby, unhappy) child squirmed in her mother's arms.

F. Circle the number of the idiom that means to suddenly become angry.

1. put up with   **2.** fly off the handle

G. Write $\underline{D}$ before the declarative sentence, $\underline{IM}$ before the imperative sentence, $\underline{E}$ before the exclamatory sentence, and $\underline{IN}$ before the interrogative sentence. Then underline the simple subject, and circle the simple predicate in each sentence.

_____ **1.** Wait until the speech is over.   _____ **3.** Ouch! I burned myself!

_____ **2.** What do you believe?   _____ **4.** That article really made me angry.

H. Write $\underline{CS}$ before the sentence that has a compound subject and $\underline{CP}$ before the sentence that has a compound predicate.

_____ **1.** He stumbled and fell on the rough ground.

_____ **2.** Carmen and José are the leading actors.

I. Write $\underline{CS}$ before the compound sentence. Write $\underline{RO}$ before the run-on sentence. Write $\underline{I}$ before the sentence that is in inverted order.

_____ **1.** Through the woods ran the frightened deer.

_____ **2.** Once she had lived in New York, she lives in Toronto now.

_____ **3.** Brenda was cold, so she built a roaring fire.

J. Put brackets around the subordinate clause, and underline the independent clause in this complex sentence. Then write $\underline{DO}$ above the direct object.

After I moved into town, I rented a beautiful new apartment.

K. Underline the common nouns, and circle the proper nouns in the sentence.

Ms. Chang rounded up the group and began the tour of the Jefferson Memorial.

L. Circle the appositive in the sentence. Underline the noun it identifies or explains.

My favorite uncle, Tom Fiske, was recently elected mayor of Greenville.

M. Write past, present, or future to show the tense of each underlined verb.

1. _____ Kathy painted one wall in her kitchen pale blue.

2. _____ Peter will call tomorrow morning at eight o'clock.

3. _____ Each morning before breakfast, Juan walks two miles.

4. _____ I will go to the library today.

N. Circle the correct verbs in each sentence.

1. There (is, are) only six weeks left before we (go, went) on vacation.

2. Steve (set, sat) down and (lay, laid) the sleeping kitten in his lap.

3. To (teach, learn) how to ski, you should (take, took) lessons.

4. (Sit, Set) the plate beside the sink where the glasses are (sitting, setting).

O. Circle the number of the sentence that is in the active voice.

1. The packages were sent two weeks ago.

2. Phillip leaped to his feet to disagree with the speaker.

P. Write SP before the sentence that has a subject pronoun, OP before the sentence that has an object pronoun, PP before the sentence that has a possessive pronoun, and IP before the sentence that has an indefinite pronoun. Circle the pronoun in each sentence.

1. _____ Nobody understands what happened.

2. _____ Ellen played the first song for him.

3. _____ The horse raised its head to look at the dog.

4. _____ He sent the memo to four people.

Q. Underline the pronoun. Circle its antecedent.

Janet and Jason met to discuss the response to their request.

R. Write adjective or adverb to describe the underlined word.

1. _____ These days are the best of the summer.

2. _____ Charlotte tiptoed quietly past the open door.

3. _____ That was the most difficult skating move I've ever seen.

4. _____ I really like Canadian bacon on my pizza.

5. _____ The dachshund is a tiny breed of dog.

6. _____ That heavy tree will be extremely hard to move.

S. Underline each prepositional phrase twice. Circle each preposition. Underline the conjunction once.

I don't have the time or the patience to talk about the complaints of those people.

T. **Rewrite the letter. Add capital letters and punctuation where needed.**

956 e. garden circle
bowman tx 78787
april 13 2005

dear steve___

    were so excited youre coming to visit___ even little scott managed to say uncle steve visit which was pretty good for a child of only twenty two months wouldnt you agree___ oh i want to be sure i have the information correct___ please let me know as soon as possible if any of this is wrong flight 561 arrives at 310 P.M. may 22 2005___ see you then___

your sister___

amanda

_____

_____

_____

_____

_____

_____

_____

_____

_____

_____

_____

_____

_____

_____

_____

_____

Check What You Know Correlation Chart

Below is a list of the sections on *Check What You Know* and the pages on which the skills in each section are taught. If you missed any questions, turn to the pages listed and practice the skills. Then correct the problems you missed on *Check What You Know*.

Section	Skill	Practice Page
	Unit 1 Vocabulary	
A	Synonyms and Antonyms	5
	Homonyms	6
B	Homographs	7
C	Prefixes	8
	Suffixes	9
	Compound Words	11
D	Contractions	10
E	Connotation/Denotation	12
F	Idioms	13
	Unit 2 Sentences	
G	Types of Sentences	19
	Simple Subjects and Predicates	22
H	Compound Subjects	24
	Compound Predicates	25
	Combining Sentences	26
I	Position of Subjects	23
	Compound and Complex Sentences	31–32
	Correcting Run-on Sentences	33
J	Direct Objects	27
	Independent and Subordinate Clauses	29
	Compound and Complex Sentences	31
	Unit 3 Grammar and Usage	
K	Common and Proper Nouns	39
L	Appositives	44
M	Verb Phrases	46
N	Using *Is/Are* and *Was/Were*	49
	Past Tenses of *See*, *Go*, and *Begin*	50
	Past Tenses of *Freeze*, *Choose*, *Speak*, and *Break*	51

Section	Skill	Practice Page
	Unit 3 Grammar and Usage	
N	*Come*, *Ring*, *Drink*, *Know*, and *Throw*	52
	Past Tenses of *Give*, *Take*, and *Write*	53
	Eat, *Fall*, *Draw*, *Drive*, and *Run*	54
	Forms of *Do*	55
	Using *May/Can* and *Teach/Learn*	62
	Using *Sit/Set* and *Lay/Lie*	63
O	Active and Passive Voice	58
P	Pronouns	64
	Demonstrative and Indefinite Pronouns	65
	Relative Pronouns	67
Q	Pronouns	64
	Antecedents	66
R	Adjectives	69
	Demonstrative Adjectives	70
	Comparing with Adjectives	71
	Adverbs	72
	Comparing with Adverbs	73
	Using Adjectives and Adverbs	74
S	Prepositions	75
	Prepositional Phrases	76
	Conjunctions	78
	Unit 4 Capitalization and Punctuation	
T	Using Capital Letters	84–85
	Using End Punctuation	86
	Using Commas	87–88
	Using Quotation Marks and Apostrophes	89
	Using Other Punctuation	90

Synonyms and Antonyms

> ■ A **synonym** is a word that has the same or nearly the same meaning as one or more other words.   EXAMPLES: reply – answer   talk – speak

A. Write a synonym for each word below.

1. pleasant _____
2. enough _____
3. leave_____
4. inquire _____

5. fearless_____
6. artificial _____
7. famous _____
8. trade _____

9. house _____
10. nation _____
11. difficult _____
12. vacant _____

B. Write four sentences about recycling. In each sentence, use a synonym for the word in parentheses. Underline the synonym.

1. (packaging) _____

2. (waste) _____

3. (landfill) _____

4. (planet) _____

> ■ An **antonym** is a word that has the opposite meaning of another word.
> EXAMPLES: old – new   bad – good

C. Write an antonym for each word below.

1. failure_____
2. absent _____
3. before _____
4. slow_____

5. all _____
6. forget _____
7. love _____
8. no _____

9. friend_____
10. always _____
11. light _____
12. forward _____

D. In each sentence, write an antonym for the word in parentheses that makes sense in the sentence.

1. Thao ran his hand along the (smooth) _____ surface of the wood.

2. He knew he would have to (stop) _____ sanding it.

3. Only after sanding would he be able to (destroy) _____ a table.

4. He would try to (forget) _____ not to sand it too much.

Homonyms

LESSON 2

> ■ A **homonym** is a word that sounds the same as another word but has a different spelling and a different meaning.
> EXAMPLES: their – they're – there   hear – here

A. Underline the correct homonym(s) in each sentence below.

1. What is the (weight, wait) of that rocket?

2. The (sale, sail) on the lake will be rough today.

3. Don't you like to (brows, browse) around in a bookstore?

4. We spent several (days, daze) at an old-fashioned (in, inn).

5. The ship was caught in an ice (flow, floe).

6. A large (boulder, bolder) rolled down the mountainside.

7. Why is that crowd on the (pier, peer)?

8. They asked the bank for a (lone, loan).

9. We drove four miles in a foggy (missed, mist).

10. Don't you like to (sea, see) a field of golden wheat?

11. Jack (threw, through) the ball (threw, through) the garage window.

12. We (buy, by) our fish from the market down on the (beach, beech).

13. The band will march down the middle (aisle, isle) of the auditorium.

14. Who is the (principal, principle) of your school?

15. The United States Congress (meats, meets) in the capitol in Washington, D.C.

16. The farmer caught the horse by the (rain, reign, rein).

17. She stepped on the (break, brake) suddenly.

18. (Their, There) are too many people to get on this boat.

19. The wren (flew, flue) in a (strait, straight) line.

20. We were not (allowed, aloud) to visit the museum yesterday.

B. Write a homonym for each word below.

1. weigh _____

2. steal _____

3. sail _____

4. fare _____

5. maid _____

6. deer _____

7. ate _____

8. vain _____

9. strait _____

10. threw _____

11. soar _____

12. bored _____

13. see _____

14. sent _____

15. pare _____

16. peace _____

17. sun _____

18. blue _____

Homographs

> ■ A **homograph** is a word that has the same spelling as another word but a different meaning and sometimes a different pronunciation.
> EXAMPLE: <u>saw</u>, meaning "have seen," and <u>saw</u>, meaning "a tool used for cutting"

A. Circle the letter for the definition that best defines each underlined homograph.

1. Sara jumped at the <u>bangs</u> of the exploding balloons.

   a. fringe of hair   **b.** loud noises

2. She grabbed a stick to <u>arm</u> herself against the threat.

   a. part of the body   **b.** take up a weapon

3. The dog's <u>bark</u> woke the family.

   a. noise a dog makes   **b.** outside covering on a tree

4. Mix the pancake <u>batter</u> for three minutes.

   a. person at bat   **b.** mixture for cooking

B. Use the homographs in the box to complete the sentences below. Each homograph will be used twice.

1. Pieces of a board game are _____.

   People who are cashiers are _____.

2. A water bird is a _____.

   To lower the head is to _____.

3. A metal container is a _____.

   If you are able, you _____.

4. To get down from something is to _____.

   If something is on fire, it is _____.

duck
alight
can
checkers

C. Write the homograph for each pair of meanings below. The first letter of each word is given for you.

1. **a.** place for horses   **b.** delay   s_____

2. **a.** a metal fastener   **b.** a sound made with fingers   s_____

3. **a.** to crush   **b.** a yellow vegetable   s_____

4. **a.** a bad doctor   **b.** the sound made by a duck   q_____

5. **a.** to strike   **b.** a party fruit drink   p_____

4 LESSON Prefixes

> ■ A **prefix** added to the beginning of a base word changes the meaning
>   of the word.
>   EXAMPLE: un-, meaning "not," + the base word <u>done</u> = <u>undone</u>,
>   meaning "not done"
> ■ Some prefixes have one meaning, and others have more than
>   one meaning.
>
> | EXAMPLES: | prefix | meaning |
> |---|---|---|
> | | im-, in-, non-, un- | not |
> | | dis-, in-, non- | opposite of, lack of, not |
> | | mis- | bad, badly, wrong, wrongly |
> | | pre- | before |
> | | re- | again |

A. Add the prefix **un-, im-, non-,** or **mis-** to the base word in parentheses. Write the new word in the sentence. Then write the definition of the new word on the line after the sentence. Use a dictionary if necessary.

1. It is _____ (practical) to put a new monkey into a cage with other monkeys.

_____

2. The monkeys might _____ (behave) with a newcomer among them.

_____

3. They will also feel quite _____ (easy) for a number of days or even weeks.

_____

4. Even if the new monkey is _____ (violent) in nature, the others may harm it.

_____

5. Sometimes animal behavior can be quite _____ (usual).

_____

B. Underline each prefix. Write the meaning of each word that has a prefix.

1. unexpected guest _____

2. really disappear _____

3. disagree often _____

4. misspell a name _____

5. preview a movie _____

6. reenter a room _____

7. misplace a shoe _____

8. impossible situation _____

9. nonstop reading _____

10. unimportant discussion _____

11. insane story _____

12. prejudge a person _____

LESSON 5 · Suffixes

■ A **suffix** added to the end of a base word changes the meaning of the word.
  EXAMPLE: -ful, meaning "full of," + the base word joy = joyful,
  meaning "full of joy"
■ Some suffixes have one meaning, and others have more than one meaning.

EXAMPLES:	**suffix**	**meaning**
	-able	able to be, suitable or inclined to
	-al	relating to, like
	-ful	as much as will fill, full of
	-less	without, that does not
	-ous	full of
	-y	having, full of

A. Add a suffix from the list above to the base word in parentheses. Write the new word. Then write the definition of the new word on the line after the sentence. Do not use any suffix more than once.

1. Switzerland is a _____ country. (mountain)

   _____

2. If you visit there, it is _____ to have a walking stick. (help)

   _____

3. Many tourists visit the country's _____ mountains to ski each year. (snow)

   _____

4. The Swiss people have a great deal of _____ pride. (nation)

   _____

5. Many Swiss are _____ about several languages. (knowledge)

   _____

B. Underline each suffix. Write the meaning of each word that has a suffix.

1. breakable toy _____

2. endless waves _____

3. hazardous path _____

4. inflatable raft _____

5. poisonous snake _____

6. dependable trains _____

7. humorous program _____

8. tearful goodbye _____

9. bumpy ride _____

10. careless driver _____

11. natural food _____

12. magical wand _____

LESSON 6

Contractions

- A **contraction** is a word formed by joining two other words.
- An **apostrophe** shows where a letter or letters have been left out.   EXAMPLE: do not = don't
- <u>Won't</u> is an exception.   EXAMPLE: will not = won't

A. Underline each contraction. Write the words that make up each contraction on the line.

1. Stingrays look as if they're part bird, part fish. _____

2. Stingrays cover themselves with sand so they won't be seen. _____

3. There's a chance that waders might step on a stingray and get stung. _____

4. That's a painful way to learn that you shouldn't forget about stingrays.

   _____   _____

5. Until recently, stingrays weren't seen very often. _____

6. It doesn't seem likely, but some stingrays will eat out of divers' hands. _____

7. Because its mouth is underneath, the stingray can't see what it's eating.

   _____   _____

8. Once they've been fed by hand, they'll flutter around for more.

   _____   _____

9. It's hard to believe these stingrays aren't afraid of humans.

   _____   _____

10. To pet a stingray, they'd gently touch its velvety skin. _____

B. Find the pairs of words that can be made into contractions. Underline each pair. Then write the contraction each word pair can make on the lines following the sentences.

1. I have never tried scuba diving, but I would like to.

   _____   _____

2. It is a good way to explore what is under the water.

   _____   _____

3. First, I will need to take lessons in the pool. _____

4. Then I can find out what to do if the equipment does not work. _____

7 LESSON

Compound words

- A **compound word** is a word that is made up of two or more words. The meaning of many compound words is related to the meaning of each individual word.

    EXAMPLE: blue + berry = blueberry, meaning "a type of berry that is blue in color"

- Compound words may be written as one word, as hyphenated words, or as two separate words. Always check a dictionary.

A. Combine the words in the list to make compound words. You may use words more than once.

| air | knob | door | port | paper | condition | black | berry |
| sand | line | stand | under | way | ground | bird | sea |

1. _____   7. _____

2. _____   8. _____

3. _____   9. _____

4. _____   10. _____

5. _____   11. _____

6. _____   12. _____

B. Answer the following questions.

1. Whirl means "to move in circles." What is a whirlpool?

_____

2. Since quick means "moves rapidly," what is quicksand?

_____

3. Rattle means "to make sharp, short sounds quickly." What is a rattlesnake?

_____

4. A ring is "a small, circular band." What is an earring?

_____

5. Pool can mean "a group of people who do something together." What is a car pool?

_____

6. A lace can be "a string or cord that is used to hold something together." What is a shoelace?

_____

Connotation/Denotation

■ The **denotation** of a word is its exact meaning as stated in a dictionary.
  EXAMPLE: The denotation of casual is "not fancy or formal."
■ The **connotation** of a word is an added meaning that suggests something positive or negative.
  EXAMPLES: **Negative:** Sloppy suggests "very messy." Sloppy has a negative connotation.
  Positive: Casual suggests "informal or relaxed." Casual has a positive connotation.
■ Some words are neutral. They do not suggest either good or bad feelings.
  EXAMPLES: calendar, toy, pencil

A. Write (–) if the word has a negative connotation. Write (+) if it has a positive connotation. Write (N) if the word is neutral.

1. _____ lazy
   _____ relaxed

2. _____ determined
   _____ stubborn

3. _____ drug
   _____ remedy

4. _____ clever
   _____ sneaky

5. _____ pretty
   _____ gorgeous

6. _____ grand
   _____ large

7. _____ old
   _____ antique

8. _____ curious
   _____ nosy

9. _____ make
   _____ create

10. _____ weird
    _____ unique

11. _____ criticize
    _____ evaluate

12. _____ snooty
    _____ refined

B. Rewrite the paragraph below. Replace the underlined words with words that do not have a negative connotation.

Jason shoved his way through the mob of people. He swaggered through the doorway and slouched against the wall. His clothes were quite gaudy. He glared at everyone with hostile eyes. Then he snickered and said in a loud tone, "I'm finally here."

_____

_____

_____

_____

_____

_____

_____

_____

Idioms

> ■ An **idiom** is an expression that has a meaning different from the usual meanings of the individual words within it.
>   EXAMPLE: <u>We're all in the same boat</u> means "We're in a similar situation," not, "We're all in a watercraft together."

A. Read each sentence. Then write the letter of the corresponding idiom for the underlined word or words.

A. shaken up	**D.** beside herself	**G.** comes through	**J.** down in the dumps
B. fly off the handle	**E.** in a bind	**H.** in the doghouse	**K.** stands up for
C. on cloud nine	**F.** put up with	**I.** on the fence	

1. One day Julia will be <u>sad</u>. _____

2. The next day you may find her <u>unbelievably happy</u>. _____

3. But be careful when Julia is <u>very scared or confused</u>. _____

4. She's liable to <u>become suddenly angry</u>. _____

5. Julia always <u>defends</u> her views, no matter what. _____

6. She won't <u>allow</u> any argument. _____

7. One time when I insisted that she listen to my viewpoint, she was <u>really upset</u>. _____

8. I was <u>out of favor</u> for weeks. _____

9. On the other hand, when a friend of Julia's is <u>in a difficult situation</u>, she really <u>helps</u>. _____ _____

10. Like a true friend, Julia is there when I am <u>unable to make a decision</u>. _____

B. For the underlined idiom in each sentence below, write the usual meaning of the words that make up the idiom.

1. Kelly can't decide whether she wants to go, so our plans are still <u>up in the air</u>. _____undecided_____

2. If I get the job, I'll be <u>walking on air</u>. _____

3. My friend's business is <u>on the skids</u>. _____

4. George's ideas are <u>off the wall</u>. _____

5. That's enough silliness. Let's <u>talk turkey</u>. _____

6. Victor was <u>in hot water</u> for not cleaning the garage. _____

7. The audience was <u>all ears</u> when you spoke. _____

8. The lost book <u>turned up</u> yesterday. _____

9. Jan and I <u>put our heads together</u> to solve the problem. _____

Review

A. Write <u>S</u> before each pair of synonyms. Write <u>A</u> before each pair of antonyms.

_____ **1.** quiet, noisy   _____ **5.** healthy, sick   _____ **9.** fast, quick

_____ **2.** fearless, brave   _____ **6.** calm, peaceful   _____ **10.** cry, weep

_____ **3.** begin, start   _____ **7.** lost, found   _____ **11.** bottom, top

_____ **4.** gentle, rough   _____ **8.** night, day   _____ **12.** dull, sharp

B. Using the homonyms in parentheses, write the correct words on the lines.

1. (week, weak) Anna was _____ for a _____ after she had the flu.

2. (right, write) Did you _____ down the _____ address?

3. (blew, blue) The wind _____ leaves and twigs into the beautiful _____ water.

4. (read, red) Meg _____ a poem about a young girl with _____ hair and freckles.

5. (pane, pain) Maria felt a _____ in her hand when she tried to remove the broken

window _____ .

C. Circle the letter of the best definition for each underlined homograph.

1. John <u>flies</u> to California every summer to visit his family.

    a. insects   **b.** moves in the air

2. Mr. Bailey owns a fruit and vegetable <u>stand</u>.

    a. to be on one's feet   **b.** a small, open structure

3. The band enjoyed performing at the <u>ball</u>.

    a. a large formal dance   **b.** a round body or object

4. Don't forget to <u>wind</u> the alarm clock before you go to bed.

    a. air movement   **b.** to tighten a spring

D. Choose an appropriate prefix or suffix from the box for each of the underlined words below. Write the new word on the line.

dis-	mis-	re-	un-	-ish	-ful	-less	-en

1. full of <u>thanks</u> _____   **5.** to make <u>black</u> in color _____

2. to <u>pay</u> again _____   **6.** without <u>thanks</u> _____

3. to not <u>agree</u> _____   **7.** not <u>happy</u> _____

4. act as a <u>fool</u> _____   **8.** <u>take</u> wrongly _____

E. Underline the pair of words that can be written as a contraction in each sentence. Then write each contraction on the line.

_____ 1. Yolanda does not want to work late today.

_____ 2. She would rather come in early tomorrow.

_____ 3. It is getting dark.

_____ 4. She does not like driving in the dark.

_____ 5. You must not blame her.

_____ 6. Who is going to stay with her?

_____ 7. James did not volunteer.

F. Combine two words in each sentence to make a compound word. Write the word on the line.

1. I polished the brass knob on the door. _____

2. Lynn rested her swollen foot on the stool. _____

3. The police tried to block the road to catch the thief. _____

4. Please walk on the left side of the street. _____

5. I keep my green plants in my warm house during the winter. _____

G. Write (–) if the underlined word has a negative connotation. Write (+) if the underlined word has a positive connotation.

_____ 1. Joe is sometimes narrow-minded.

_____ 2. Marie is very outgoing.

_____ 3. Do you like to gossip?

_____ 4. Carla can gab for hours.

_____ 5. Let's donate this later.

_____ 6. The child grabbed the toy and ran away.

_____ 7. Those insects are real pests.

_____ 8. I demand that you listen to me.

_____ 9. The mansion was very old.

_____ 10. Steve drives an old jalopy.

H. Underline the idiom in each sentence. Then write what the idiom means.

1. Since there was little time, the mayor only hit the high spots of his speech.

_____

2. The committee's bank account was low, so they had to cut corners on their party.

_____

3. Mark couldn't find a job, so he asked his uncle to pull some strings for him.

_____

Using What You've Learned

A. Rewrite the following sentences, using synonyms for the underlined words.

1. The lightning flashed across the black sky as the trees bent in the wind.

   _____

2. Blasts of wind whistled through the openings between the boards on the window.

   _____

3. Then a hush seemed to fall over our part of the world.

   _____

B. Rewrite the following sentences, using antonyms for the underlined words.

1. Before the storm hit, the sky got darker.

   _____

2. Black clouds drifted across the evening sky.

   _____

3. The heavy wind was blowing leaves over the trees.

   _____

C. Write a sentence using a homonym for each word.

1. new _____

2. grater _____

3. choose _____

4. weight _____

5. waist _____

D. For each homograph below, write two sentences. Be sure to use a different meaning of the homograph in each sentence.

1. light   a. _____

           b. _____

2. shed   a. _____

           b. _____

3. rest   a. _____

           b. _____

E. Add one of the following prefixes or suffixes to each base word to make a new word.

> **Prefixes:** in-, non-, dis-, mis-, pre-, re-
> **Suffixes:** -able, -ful, -less

1. place _____
2. direct _____
3. use _____
4. measure _____
5. speech _____

6. tire _____
7. remark _____
8. spell _____
9. pay _____
10. fund _____

F. Use the following idioms in sentences. Use a dictionary if necessary.

1. throw in the towel _____
2. pulling my leg _____
3. skating on thin ice _____
4. get in touch with _____
5. keep an eye on _____

G. Think of words that have almost the same meaning as the neutral word, but have a more negative or positive connotation. Complete the chart with your words.

Negative Connotation	Neutral	Positive Connotation
1. _____	wet	_____
2. _____	shout	_____
3. _____	thin	_____
4. _____	old	_____
5. _____	talk	_____
6. _____	clothes	_____
7. _____	ask	_____
8. _____	work	_____
9. _____	cut	_____
10. _____	eat	_____

Recognizing Sentences

> ■ A **sentence** is a group of words that expresses a complete thought.
>   EXAMPLE: Marie sings well.

■ **Some of the following groups of words are sentences, and some are not. Write S before each group that is a sentence. Punctuate each sentence with a period.**

_____ 1. When the downhill skiing season begins____

_____ 2. Last summer I visited my friend in New Jersey____

_____ 3. From the very beginning of the first-aid lessons____

_____ 4. One of the children from the neighborhood____

_____ 5. A visiting musician played the organ____

_____ 6. On the way to school this morning____

_____ 7. "I love you, Mother," said Mike____

_____ 8. The blue house at the corner of Maple Street____

_____ 9. After Emily left, the phone rang off the hook____

_____ 10. Speak distinctly and loudly so that you can be heard____

_____ 11. I have finally learned to drive our car____

_____ 12. This is William's tenth birthday____

_____ 13. At the very last moment, we were ready____

_____ 14. When you speak in front of people____

_____ 15. The basket of fruit on the table____

_____ 16. Please answer the telephone, Julia____

_____ 17. Hurrying to class because he is late____

_____ 18. The first thing in the morning____

_____ 19. That mistake was costly and unfortunate____

_____ 20. We are planning to build a new doghouse____

_____ 21. The dog chased the cat up the tree____

_____ 22. Daniel Boone was born in Pennsylvania____

_____ 23. The giant cottonwood in our backyard____

_____ 24. Marla, bring my notebook____

_____ 25. On a stool beside the back door____

_____ 26. Sometimes the noise from the street____

_____ 27. Somewhere out of state____

_____ 28. The band played a lively march____

_____ 29. That flight arrived on time____

_____ 30. Was cracked in dozens of places____

Types of Sentences

> - A **declarative sentence** makes a statement. It is followed by a period (.).   EXAMPLE: Alicia is my cousin.
> - An **interrogative sentence** asks a question. It is followed by a question mark (?).   EXAMPLE: Where are you going?
> - An **imperative sentence** expresses a command or request. It is followed by a period (.).   EXAMPLE: Close the door.
> - An **exclamatory sentence** expresses strong emotion. It can also express a command or request that is made with great excitement. It is followed by an exclamation mark (!).   EXAMPLES: How you frightened me! Look at that accident!

- Write **D** for declarative, **IN** for interrogative, **IM** for imperative, or **E** for exclamatory before each sentence. Put the correct punctuation at the end of each sentence.

_____ 1. Everyone will be here by nine o'clock____

_____ 2. Train your mind to do its work efficiently____

_____ 3. How does a canal lock work____

_____ 4. Prepare each day's assignment on time____

_____ 5. Are we going to the game now____

_____ 6. Who brought these delicious peaches____

_____ 7. Our guests have arrived____

_____ 8. What is meant by rotation of crops____

_____ 9. Please bring a glass of water____

_____ 10. Stop that noise____

_____ 11. Always stand erect____

_____ 12. Who arranged these flowers____

_____ 13. Anna, what do you have in that box____

_____ 14. The Vikings were famous sailors____

_____ 15. Have you solved all the problems in our lesson____

_____ 16. Jack, hand me that wrench____

_____ 17. What is the capital of California____

_____ 18. Cultivate a pleasant manner____

_____ 19. How is a pizza made____

_____ 20. Block that kick____

_____ 21. A nation is measured by the character of its people____

_____ 22. Are you an early riser____

_____ 23. Practice good table manners____

Complete Subjects and Predicates

- Every sentence has two main parts, a **complete subject** and a **complete predicate**.
- The complete subject includes all the words that tell who or what the sentence is about.
  EXAMPLES: **My brother**/likes to go with us. **Six geese**/honked loudly.
- The complete predicate includes all the words that state the action or condition of the subject.
  EXAMPLES: My brother/**likes to go with us**. Six geese/**honked loudly**.

A. Draw a line between the complete subject and the complete predicate in each sentence.

1. Bees/fly.

2. Trains whistle.

3. A talented artist drew this cartoon.

4. The wind blew furiously.

5. My grandmother made this dress last year.

6. We surely have enjoyed the holiday.

7. These cookies are made with rice.

8. This letter came to the post office box.

9. They rent a cabin in Colorado every summer.

10. Jennifer is reading about the pioneer days in the West.

11. Our baseball team won the third game of the series.

12. The band played a cheerful tune.

13. A cloudless sky is a great help to a pilot.

14. The voice of the auctioneer was heard throughout the hall.

15. A sudden flash of lightning startled us.

16. The wind howled down the chimney.

17. Paul's dog followed him to the grocery store.

18. Their apartment is on the sixth floor.

19. We have studied many interesting places.

20. Each player on the team deserves credit for the victory.

21. Forest rangers fought the raging fire.

22. A friend taught Robert a valuable lesson.

23. Millions of stars make up the Milky Way.

24. The airplane was lost in the thick clouds.

25. Many of the children waded in the pool.

26. Yellowstone Park is a large national park.

27. Cold weather is predicted for tomorrow.

28. The trees were covered with moss.

B. Write a sentence by adding a complete predicate to each complete subject.

1. All of the students _____

2. Elephants _____

3. The top of the mountain _____

4. The television programs tonight _____

5. I _____

6. Each of the girls _____

7. My father's truck _____

8. The dam across the river _____

9. Our new station wagon _____

10. You _____

11. The books in our bookcase _____

12. The mountains _____

13. Today's paper _____

14. The magazine staff _____

C. Write a sentence by adding a complete subject to each complete predicate.

1. _____ is the largest city in Mexico.

2. _____ came to our program.

3. _____ is a valuable mineral.

4. _____ grow beside the road.

5. _____ traveled day and night.

6. _____ was a great inventor.

7. _____ wrote the letter of complaint.

8. _____ met us at the airport.

9. _____ made ice cream for the picnic.

10. _____ made a nest in our tree.

11. _____ lives near the shopping center.

12. _____ have a meeting on Saturday.

Simple Subjects and Predicates

> - The **simple subject** of a sentence is the main word in the complete subject. The simple subject is a noun or a word that stands for a noun.
>   EXAMPLE: My **sister**/lost her gloves.
> - Sometimes the simple subject is also the complete subject.
>   EXAMPLE: **She**/lost her gloves.
> - The **simple predicate** of a sentence is a verb within the complete predicate. The simple predicate may be a one-word verb or a verb of more than one word.
>   EXAMPLES: She/**lost** her gloves. She/**is looking** for them.

- **Draw a line between the complete subject and complete predicate in each sentence below. Underline the simple subject once and the simple predicate twice.**

1. A sudden clap of thunder/frightened all of us.

2. The soft snow covered the fields and roads.

3. We drove very slowly over the narrow bridge.

4. The students are making an aquarium.

5. Our class read about the founder of Hull House.

6. The women were talking in the park.

7. This album has many folk songs.

8. We are furnishing the sandwiches for tonight's picnic.

9. All the trees on that lawn are giant oaks.

10. Many Americans are working in foreign countries.

11. The manager read the names of the contest winners.

12. Bill brought these large melons.

13. We opened the front door of the house.

14. The two mechanics worked on the car for an hour.

15. Black and yellow butterflies fluttered among the flowers.

16. The child spoke politely.

17. We found many beautiful shells along the shore.

18. The best part of the program is the dance number.

19. Every ambitious person is working hard.

20. Sheryl swam across the lake two times.

21. Our program will begin promptly at eight o'clock.

22. The handle of this basket is broken.

23. The clock in the tower strikes every hour.

24. The white farmhouse on that road belongs to my cousin.

25. The first game of the season will be played tomorrow.

14 LESSON

Position of Subjects

- When the subject of a sentence comes before the verb, the sentence is in **natural order.** EXAMPLE: Henry went to the park.
- When the verb or part of the verb comes before the subject, the sentence is in **inverted order.** EXAMPLES: Here are the calculators. Down came the rain.
- Many questions are in inverted order. EXAMPLE: Where is the restaurant?
- Sometimes the subject of a sentence is not expressed, as in a command or request. The understood subject is you. EXAMPLES: Call about the job now. (You) call about the job now.

■ **Rewrite each inverted sentence in natural order. Underline the simple subject once and the simple predicate twice. Add you as the subject to commands or requests.**

1. When is the movie playing?

_____

2. Never will I forget my first train trip.

_____

3. Here is the picture I want to buy.

_____

4. Seldom has he been ill.

_____

5. Out went the lights.

_____

6. There were bookcases on all sides of the room.

_____

7. Take the roast from the oven.

_____

8. Around the sharp curve swerved the speeding car.

_____

9. Get out of the swimming pool.

_____

10. Study for the spelling test.

_____

11. There are two children in the pool.

_____

15 Compound Subjects
LESSON

■ A **compound subject** is made up of two or more simple subjects.
EXAMPLE: **Henri** and **Tanya** / are tall people.

A. Draw a line between the complete subject and the complete predicate in each sentence. Write <u>SS</u> for a simple subject. Write <u>CS</u> for a compound subject.

<u>CS</u>   **1.** Arturo and I/often work late on Friday.

_____   **2.** Sandy left the person near the crowded exit.

_____   **3.** She and I will mail the packages to San Francisco, California, today.

_____   **4.** Shanghai and New Delhi are two cities visited by the group.

_____   **5.** The fire spread rapidly to other buildings in the neighborhood.

_____   **6.** Luis and Lenora helped their parents with the chores.

_____   **7.** Swimming, jogging, and hiking were our favorite sports.

_____   **8.** Melbourne and Sydney are important Australian cities.

_____   **9.** Eric and I had an interesting experience Saturday.

_____   **10.** The Red Sea and the Mediterranean Sea are connected by the Suez Canal.

_____   **11.** The Republicans and the Democrats made many speeches before the election.

_____   **12.** The people waved to us from the top of the cliff.

_____   **13.** Liz and Jim crated the freshly-picked apples.

_____   **14.** Clean clothes and a neat appearance are important in an interview.

_____   **15.** The kitten and the old dog are good friends.

_____   **16.** David and Paul are on their way to the swimming pool.

_____   **17.** Tom combed his dog's shiny black coat.

_____   **18.** Redbud and dogwood trees bloom in the spring.

_____   **19.** I hummed a cheerful tune on the way to the meeting.

_____   **20.** Buffalo, deer, and antelope once roamed the plains of North America.

_____   **21.** Gina and Hiroshi raked the leaves.

_____   **22.** Brasília and São Paulo are two cities in Brazil.

_____   **23.** Hang gliding is a popular sport in Hawaii.

_____   **24.** Our class went on a field trip to the aquarium.

_____   **25.** The doctor asked him to get a blood test.

B. Write two sentences containing compound subjects.

1. _____

2. _____

16 LESSON

Compound Predicates

■ A **compound predicate** is made up of two or more simple predicates.
EXAMPLE: Joseph / **dances** and **sings**.

A. Draw a line between the complete subject and the complete predicate in each sentence. Write SP for each simple predicate. Write CP for each compound predicate.

__CP__ 1. Edward / grinned and nodded.

_____ 2. Plants need air to live.

_____ 3. Old silver tea kettles were among their possessions.

_____ 4. My sister buys and sells real estate.

_____ 5. Snow covered every highway in the area.

_____ 6. Mr. Sanders designs and makes odd pieces of furniture.

_____ 7. Popcorn is one of my favorite snack foods.

_____ 8. Soccer is one of my favorite sports.

_____ 9. The ducks quickly crossed the road and found the ducklings.

_____ 10. They came early and stayed late.

_____ 11. Crystal participated in the Special Olympics this year.

_____ 12. José raked and sacked the leaves.

_____ 13. Perry built the fire and cooked supper.

_____ 14. We collected old newspapers for the recycling center.

_____ 15. Doug arrived in Toronto, Ontario, during the afternoon.

_____ 16. Tony's parents are visiting in Oregon and Washington.

_____ 17. The Garzas live in that apartment building on Oak Street.

_____ 18. The shingles were picked up and delivered today.

_____ 19. The audience talked and laughed before the performance.

_____ 20. Automobiles crowd and jam that highway early in the morning.

_____ 21. The apples are rotting in the boxes.

_____ 22. The leader of the group grumbled and scolded.

_____ 23. She worked hard and waited patiently.

_____ 24. Nelson Mandela is a great civil rights activist.

_____ 25. The supervisor has completed the work for the week.

B. Write two sentences containing compound predicates.

1. _____

2. _____

Combining Sentences

> - Two sentences in which the subjects are different and the predicates are the same can be combined into one sentence. The two subjects are joined by and.   EXAMPLE: **Hurricanes** are storms. **Tornadoes** are storms. **Hurricanes and tornadoes** are storms.
> - Two sentences in which the subjects are the same and the predicates are different can be combined into one sentence. The two predicates may be joined by or, and, or but.   EXAMPLE: Hurricanes **begin over tropical oceans.** Hurricanes **move inland.** Hurricanes **begin over tropical oceans and move inland.**

- **Combine each pair of sentences below. Underline the compound subject or the compound predicate in each sentence that you write.**

1. Lightning is part of a thunderstorm. Thunder is part of a thunderstorm.

   _____

2. Thunderstorms usually happen in the spring. Thunderstorms bring heavy rains.

   _____

3. Depending on how close or far away it is, thunder sounds like a sharp crack.
   Depending on how close or far away it is, thunder rumbles.

   _____

   _____

4. Lightning is very exciting to watch. Lightning can be very dangerous.

   _____

5. Lightning causes many fires. Lightning harms many people.

   _____

6. An open field is an unsafe place to be during a thunderstorm.
   A golf course is an unsafe place to be during a thunderstorm.

   _____

   _____

7. Benjamin Franklin wanted to protect people from lightning.
   Benjamin Franklin invented the lightning rod.

   _____

   _____

8. A lightning rod is a metal rod placed on the top of a building.
   A lightning rod is connected to the ground by a cable.

   _____

   _____

18 LESSON Direct Objects

> ■ The **direct object** tells who or what receives the action of the verb. The direct object is a noun or pronoun that follows an action verb.
>
> EXAMPLE: Those countries export **coffee**.
> (DO above **coffee**)

■ **Underline the verb in each sentence. Then write DO above each direct object.**

1. Juanita's good driving prevented an accident.

2. Every person should have an appreciation of music.

3. Gene, pass the potatoes, please.

4. Do not waste your time on this project.

5. James, did you keep those coupons?

6. Geraldo collects foreign stamps.

7. Eli Whitney invented the cotton gin.

8. Answer my question.

9. We are picking trophies for our bowling league.

10. Who invented the steamboat?

11. I am reading Hemingway's *The Old Man and the Sea.*

12. The North Star guides sailors.

13. The Phoenicians gave the alphabet to civilization.

14. Every person should study world history.

15. Who made this cake?

16. Can you find a direct object in this sentence?

17. Who wrote the story of Johnny Tremain?

18. We bought several curios for our friends.

19. Tamara read the minutes of our last club meeting.

20. Did you ever make a time budget of your own?

21. Mountains have often affected the history of a nation.

22. Emma and Joe baked a pie.

19 LESSON

Indirect Objects

> - The **indirect object** is the noun or pronoun that tells to whom or for whom an action is done. In order to have an indirect object, a sentence must have a direct object.
> - The indirect object is usually placed between the action verb and the direct object.
>   EXAMPLE: Who sold **you** that fantastic **bike?**
>   (IO above you, DO above bike)

■ **Underline the verb in each sentence. Then write DO above the direct object and IO above the indirect object.**

1. Certain marine plants <u>give</u> the Red Sea its color.
   (IO above the Red Sea, DO above color)

2. I gave the cashier a check for twenty dollars.

3. The magician showed the audience a few of her tricks.

4. The coach taught them the rules of the game.

5. Roberto brought us some foreign coins.

6. This interesting book will give every reader pleasure.

7. Have you written your brother a letter?

8. They made us some sandwiches to take on our hike.

9. The astronaut gave Mission Control the data.

10. I bought my friend an etching at the art exhibit.

11. James, did you sell Mike your car?

12. We have given the dog a thorough scrubbing.

13. Give the usher your ticket.

14. Carl brought my brother a gold ring from Mexico.

15. Hand me a pencil, please.

16. The conductor gave the orchestra a short break.

17. Show me the picture of your boat.

18. I have given you my money.

19. Give Lee this message.

20. The club gave the town a new statue.

Independent and Subordinate Clauses

LESSON 20

> ■ A **clause** is a group of words that contains a subject and a predicate. There are two kinds of clauses: **independent clauses** and **subordinate clauses.**
>
> ■ An **independent clause** can stand alone as a sentence because it expresses a complete thought.
>> EXAMPLE: **The students came in** when the bell rang. **The students came in.**

A. Underline the independent clause in each sentence below.

1. Frank will be busy because he is studying.

2. I have only one hour that I can spare.

3. The project must be finished when I get back.

4. Gloria volunteered to do the typing that needs to be done.

5. The work is going too slowly for us to finish on time.

6. Before Nathan started to help, I didn't think we could finish.

7. What else should we do before we relax?

8. Since you forgot to give this page to Gloria, you can type it.

9. After she had finished typing, we completed the project.

10. We actually got it finished before the deadline.

> ■ A **subordinate clause** has a subject and predicate but cannot stand alone as a sentence because it does not express a complete thought. A subordinate clause must be combined with an independent clause to make a sentence.
>> EXAMPLE: The stamp **that I bought** was already in my collection.

B. Underline the subordinate clause in each sentence below.

1. The people who went shopping found a great sale.

2. Tony's bike, which is a mountain bike, came from that store.

3. Juana was sad when the sale was over.

4. Marianne was excited because she wanted some new things.

5. Thomas didn't find anything since he went late.

6. The mall where we went shopping was new.

7. The people who own the stores are proud of the beautiful setting.

8. The mall, which is miles away, is serviced by the city bus.

9. We ran as fast as we could because the bus was coming.

10. We were panting because we had run fast.

21 Adjective and Adverb Clauses

- An **adjective clause** is a subordinate clause that modifies a noun or a pronoun. It answers the adjective question <u>Which one?</u> or <u>What kind?</u> It usually modifies the word directly preceding it. Most adjective clauses begin with a **relative pronoun.** A relative pronoun relates an adjective clause to the noun or pronoun that the clause modifies. <u>Who</u>, <u>whom</u>, <u>whose</u>, <u>which</u>, and <u>that</u> are relative pronouns.

    EXAMPLE: Always do the work **that is assigned to you.**
    adjective clause

- An **adverb clause** is a subordinate clause that modifies a verb, an adjective, or another adverb. It answers the adverb question <u>How?</u> <u>Under what condition?</u> or <u>Why?</u> Words that introduce adverb clauses are called **subordinating conjunctions.** The many subordinating conjunctions include such words as <u>when</u>, <u>after</u>, <u>before</u>, <u>since</u>, <u>although</u>, and <u>because</u>.

    EXAMPLE: We left **when the storm clouds gathered.**
    adverb clause

A. Underline the subordinate clause. Then write <u>adjective</u> or <u>adverb</u> on the line.

_____ 1. John Paul Jones was a hero whose bravery won many victories.

_____ 2. The person who reads the most books will get a prize.

_____ 3. He overslept because he hadn't set the alarm.

_____ 4. Give a rousing cheer when our team comes off the field.

_____ 5. The parrot repeats many things that he hears.

_____ 6. The picnic that we planned was canceled.

B. Add a subordinate clause beginning with the word in parentheses to each independent clause below.

1. The package was gone   (when) _____

    _____

2. A depot is a place   (where) _____

    _____

3. Brad and I cannot go now   (because) _____

    _____

4. Tell me the name of the person   (who) _____

    _____

30

22 Compound and Complex Sentences

> - A **compound sentence** consists of two or more independent clauses. Each independent clause in a compound sentence can stand alone as a separate sentence. The independent clauses are usually joined by and, but, so, or, for, or yet and a comma.
>   EXAMPLE: I like to dance, but Jim likes to sing.
> - Sometimes a **semicolon (;)** is used to join the independent clauses in a compound sentence.
>   EXAMPLE: I like to dance; Jim likes to sing.
> - A **complex sentence** consists of one independent clause and one or more subordinate clauses.
>   EXAMPLE: **When the fire alarm went off,** everyone left the building.
>   subordinate clause

A. Write CP before each compound sentence. Write CX before each complex sentence.

_____ 1. Our team didn't always win, but we always tried to be good sports.

_____ 2. You may stay, but I am going home.

_____ 3. The rangers who serve in Yellowstone Park know every inch of the ground.

_____ 4. That statement may be correct, but it isn't very polite.

_____ 5. We will meet whenever we can.

_____ 6. The pass was thrown perfectly, but Carlos was too well guarded to catch it.

_____ 7. The toga was worn by ancient Roman youths when they reached the age of twelve.

_____ 8. That song, which is often heard on the radio, was written years ago.

_____ 9. They cannot come for dinner, but they will be here later.

_____ 10. My brother likes dogs, but I prefer cats.

_____ 11. The engine is the heart of the submarine, and the periscope is the eye.

_____ 12. I will call you when it arrives.

_____ 13. Those people who camped here were messy.

_____ 14. Edison was only thirty years old when he invented the talking machine.

_____ 15. She crept silently, for she was afraid.

_____ 16. Move the table, but be careful with it.

_____ 17. Bolivia is the only South American country that does not have a port.

_____ 18. How many stars were in the flag that Key saw "by the dawn's early light"?

_____ 19. The octopus gets its name from two Greek words that mean eight and feet.

_____ 20. You may place the order, but we cannot guarantee shipment.

_____ 21. After the sun set, we built a campfire.

_____ 22. We made hamburgers for dinner, and then we toasted marshmallows.

_____ 23. Some people sang songs; others played games.

_____ 24. When it started to rain, everyone took shelter in their tents.

B. Put brackets [ ] around the independent clauses in each compound sentence below. Then underline the simple subject once and the simple predicate twice in each clause.

1. [The streets are filled with cars], but [the sidewalks are empty].

2. Those apples are too sour to eat, but those pears are perfect.

3. She studies hard, but she saves some time to enjoy herself.

4. They lost track of time, so they were late.

5. Eric had not studied, so he failed the test.

6. Yesterday it rained all day, but today the sun is shining.

7. I set the alarm to get up early, but I couldn't get up.

8. They may sing and dance until dawn, but they will be exhausted.

9. My friend moved to Texas, and I will miss her.

10. They arrived at the theater early, but there was still a long line.

11. Lisa took her dog to the veterinarian, but his office was closed.

12. The black cat leaped, but fortunately it didn't catch the bird.

13. I found a baseball in the bushes, and I gave it to my brother.

14. We loaded the cart with groceries, and we went to the checkout.

15. The stadium was showered with lights, but the stands were empty.

16. The small child whimpered, and her mother hugged her.

17. The dark clouds rolled in, and then it began to rain.

C. In each complex sentence below, underline the subordinate clause.

1. The hummingbird is the only bird that can fly backward.

2. The cat that is sitting in the window is mine.

3. The car that is parked outside is new.

4. Jack, who is a football star, is class president.

5. Bonnie, who is an artist, is also studying computer science.

6. John likes food that is cooked in the microwave.

7. The composer who wrote the music comes from Germany.

8. We missed seeing him because we were late.

9. When Jake arrives, we will tell him what happened.

10. She walked slowly because she had hurt her leg.

11. When she walked to the podium, everyone applauded.

12. If animals could talk, they might have a lot to tell.

13. Many roads that were built in our city are no longer traveled.

14. My address book, which is bright red, is gone.

15. Ann, who is from Geórgia, just started working here today.

16. The crowd cheered when the player came to bat.

17. When he hit the ball, everyone cheered.

Correcting Run-on Sentences

> - Two or more independent clauses that are run together without the correct punctuation are called a **run-on sentence.**
>   EXAMPLE: The music was deafening I turned down the volume.
> - One way to correct a run-on sentence is to separate it into two sentences.
>   EXAMPLE: The music was deafening. I turned down the volume.
> - Another way to correct a run-on sentence is to make it into a compound sentence.
>   EXAMPLE: The music was deafening, so I turned down the volume.
> - Another way to correct a run-on sentence is to use a semicolon.
>   EXAMPLE: The music was deafening; I turned down the volume.

- **Correct each run-on sentence below by writing it as two sentences or as a compound sentence.**

1. The city council held a meeting a meeting is held every month.

   _____

   _____

2. The council members are elected by the voters there are two thousand voters in the city.

   _____

   _____

3. There is one council member from each suburb, the president is elected by the council members.

   _____

   _____

4. Those who run for office must give speeches, the speeches should be short.

   _____

   _____

5. The council decides on many activities every activity is voted on.

   _____

   _____

6. Money is needed for many of the special activities, the council also plans fund-raisers in the city.

   _____

   _____

7. The annual city picnic is sponsored by the city council the picnic is in May.

   _____

   _____

24 LESSON

Expanding Sentences

> ■ Sentences can be **expanded** by adding details to make them clearer and more interesting.   EXAMPLE: The dog ran. The **big black** dog ran **barking into the street.**
> ■ Details added to sentences may answer these questions: When? Where? How? How often? To what degree? What kind? Which? How many?

A. Expand each sentence below by adding details to answer the questions shown in parentheses. Write the expanded sentence on the line.

1. The crew was ready for liftoff.   (Which? When?)

_____

2. The shuttle was launched.   (What kind? Where?)

_____

3. The engines roared.   (How many? To what degree?)

_____

4. The spacecraft shot up.   (How? Where?)

_____

5. The astronauts studied the control panels.   (How many? Where?)

_____

B. Decide how each of the following sentences can be expanded. Write your expanded sentence on the line.

1. The singer ran onto the stage.

_____

2. The fans leaped up and cheered.

_____

3. She began to sing.

_____

4. She strummed the guitar.

_____

5. The loudspeakers blared.

_____

6. The fans began dancing.

_____

Review

A. Label each sentence as follows: Write **D** for declarative, **IN** for interrogative, **IM** for imperative, or **E** for exclamatory. Write **X̄** if it is not a sentence. Punctuate each sentence correctly.

_____ 1. Did you forget our appointment____

_____ 2. Be careful____

_____ 3. Rolled up our sleeping bags____

_____ 4. All members will meet in this room____

_____ 5. Help, I'm frightened____

_____ 6. Where are you going____

_____ 7. Oh, look out ____

_____ 8. People from all over the world____

_____ 9. Julie ran two miles____

_____ 10. Place the books here____

B. In each sentence below, underline the words that are identified in parentheses.

1. (complete subject)   The lights around the public square went out.

2. (simple subject)   Stations are in all parts of our country.

3. (direct object)   Carmen collects fans for a hobby.

4. (complete predicate)   We drove slowly across the bridge.

5. (simple predicate)   We saw an unusual flower.

6. (compound predicate)   Taro swims and dives quite well.

7. (compound subject)   The cake and bread are kept in the box.

8. (indirect object)   The referee gave our team a fifteen-yard penalty.

9. (direct object)   A good citizen obeys the laws, but a bad citizen doesn't.

10. (indirect object)   Please lend me your raincoat, so I can stay dry.

C. Write **CP** after each compound sentence and **CX** after each complex sentence.

1. The food that is needed will be bought. _____

2. Mary will get lettuce, but we may have some. _____

3. Jack, who said he would help, is late. _____

4. We will go, and they will meet us. _____

5. Jack will drive his car after it has been repaired. _____

6. We are going to Spruce Park since it is on a lake. _____

7. There are canoes that can be rented. _____

8. We can row around the lake, or we can go swimming. _____

9. We can decide what we want to do after we eat our picnic lunch. _____

10. Spruce Park is a great place, and we are going to have a wonderful time. _____

D. **Underline the verb in each sentence. Then write DO above the direct object and IO above the indirect object.**

1. The director gave the actors a new script.

2. Jenny showed her friends her vacation slides.

3. Ms. Lopez took her sick neighbor some chicken soup.

4. We handed the cashier our money.

5. Enrique, please give your brother his jacket.

E. **Underline the independent clause, and circle the subordinate clause in each sentence.**

1. The campers got wet when it started raining.

2. The candidates that I voted for in the election won easily.

3. Before the board voted on the issue, it held public hearings.

4. The freeway through town is a road where vehicles often speed.

5. While we waited, the children kept us entertained.

F. **Underline the subordinate clause in each sentence. Write adjective clause or adverb clause on the line after each sentence.**

1. Meteorologists are people who are trained in weather forecasting. _____

2. Before I decided on a college, I did many hours of research. _____

3. The experiment that I designed failed completely. _____

4. Although the furniture was old, it was very comfortable. _____

5. Many people exercise because they want to stay healthy. _____

6. I ate breakfast before I left. _____

G. **Rewrite each sentence in natural order.**

1. Just below the surface lay a large goldfish.

   _____

2. Over the roof flew the baseball.

   _____

H. **Combine each pair of sentences to form a compound sentence.**

1. Dogs are Erica's favorite animal. Cats are John's favorite animal.

   _____

2. The water reflected the sun. We put on our sunglasses.

   _____

Using What You've Learned

A. Read the sentences in the box. Then answer the questions below.

> **A.** Did I give you the tickets for the show?
> **B.** This compact disc is fantastic!
> **C.** Be at my house by seven o'clock.
> **D.** You and I can ride downtown together.
> **E.** We can stop and eat before the show.

1. _____ Which sentence has a compound subject?
2. _____ Which sentence has a compound predicate?
3. _____ Which sentence has a direct object?
4. _____ Which sentence has an indirect object?

5. _____ Which sentence is interrogative?
6. _____ Which sentences are declarative?
7. _____ Which sentence is exclamatory?
8. _____ Which sentence is imperative?

9. What is the complete subject of E? _____

10. What is the simple subject of E? _____

11. What is the complete predicate of C? _____

B. Underline the independent clause, and circle the subordinate clause in each complex sentence below.

1. The streamers sagged after we hung them.
2. Mark knows party planning because he has many parties.
3. Everyone who wants to go to the party must bring something.
4. If everyone brings something, the party will be great.
5. Unless I am wrong, the party is tomorrow.
6. As if everything had been done, Jake ran out of the room.
7. The girls who planned the party received roses.
8. I will never forget the day that I fell on my face at a party.

C. Combine each pair of sentences below to form a compound sentence.

1. The team sat in the dugout. The fans sat in the stands.

_____

2. The rain finally stopped. The game continued.

_____

3. It was the bottom of the ninth inning. There were two outs.

_____

4. The batter swung at the pitch. The umpire called, "Strike three!"

_____

D. Rewrite each inverted sentence below in natural order.

1. Reported on a television bulletin was the news of the storm.

_____

2. Into the hangar taxied the small airplane.

_____

3. Down the ramp came the tired passengers.

_____

E. Create complex sentences by adding a subordinate clause or an independent clause to each group of words.

1. She looked sad _____

2. When she thought about what she said _____

3. This was the time _____

4. After she wrote her apology _____

5. When she wrote it _____

6. Before we left the house _____

F. Rewrite the paragraph below, correcting the run-on sentences.

   In space medicine research, new types of miniature equipment for checking how the body functions have been developed on the spacecraft, astronauts' breathing rates, heartbeats, and blood pressure are taken with miniature devices no larger than a pill. These devices detect the information and transmit it to scientists back on Earth they allow the scientists to monitor astronauts' body responses from a long distance and over long periods of time.

_____

_____

_____

_____

_____

G. Read the two sentences below. Then expand each sentence by adding details to make the sentence clearer and more interesting.

1. The acrobats climbed the ladder.

_____

2. They began their act.

_____

25 LESSON

Common and Proper Nouns

- There are two main classes of nouns: **common** and **proper nouns.**
- A **common noun** names any one of a class of objects.
  EXAMPLES: woman, city, tree
- A **proper noun** names a particular person, place, or thing. It begins with a capital letter.
  EXAMPLES: Ms. Patel, Chicago, Empire State Building

A. **Underline each noun. Then write C or P above it to show whether it is a common or proper noun.**

    P   C
1. Maria is my sister.

2. Honolulu is the chief city and capital of Hawaii.

3. Rainbow Natural Bridge is hidden away in the wild mountainous part of southern Utah.

4. The Declaration of Independence is often called the birth certificate of the United States.

5. Abraham Lincoln, Edgar Allan Poe, and Frederic Chopin were born in the same year.

B. **Write a proper noun suggested by each common noun.**

1. country _____

2. book _____

3. governor _____

4. state _____

5. athlete _____

6. school _____

7. actor _____

8. day _____

9. car _____

10. lake _____

11. singer _____

12. holiday _____

13. newspaper _____

14. river _____

C. **Write a sentence using each proper noun and the common noun for its class.**

1. Mexico   Mexico is another country in North America._____

2. December _____

3. Alaska _____

4. Thanksgiving Day _____

5. Bill Clinton _____

6. Tuesday _____

26 LESSON

Concrete, Abstract, and Collective Nouns

- A **concrete noun** names things you can see and touch.
    EXAMPLES: apple, dog, fork, book, computer
- An **abstract noun** names an idea, quality, action, or feeling.
    EXAMPLES: bravery, wickedness, goodness
- A **collective noun** names a group of persons or things.
    EXAMPLES: crowd, congress, public, United States

- **Classify each common noun as concrete, collective, or abstract.**

1. humor _____
2. kindness _____
3. army _____
4. danger _____
5. committee _____
6. towel _____
7. jury _____
8. audience _____
9. bird _____
10. orchestra _____
11. fear _____
12. family _____
13. happiness _____
14. truck _____
15. team _____
16. honesty _____
17. bracelet _____
18. society _____
19. album _____
20. courage _____
21. faculty _____

22. club _____
23. photograph _____
24. poverty _____
25. class _____
26. swarm _____
27. table _____
28. goodness _____
29. flock _____
30. radio _____
31. mob _____
32. patience _____
33. herd _____
34. banana _____
35. staff _____
36. mercy _____
37. calculator _____
38. coyote _____
39. generosity _____
40. scissors _____
41. sorrow _____
42. independence _____

Singular and Plural Nouns

The following chart shows how to change **singular nouns** into **plural nouns.**		
Noun	**Plural Form**	**Examples**
Most nouns	Add -s	ship, ships nose, noses
Nouns ending in a consonant and -y	Change the -y to -i, and add -es	sky, skies navy, navies
Nouns ending in -o	Add -s or -es	hero, heroes piano, pianos
Most nouns ending in -f or -fe	Change the -f or -fe to -ves	half, halves
Most nouns ending in -ch, -sh, -s, or -x	Add -es	bench, benches bush, bushes tax, taxes
Many two-word or three-word compound nouns	Add -s to the principle word	son-in-law, sons-in-law
Nouns with the same form in the singular and plural	No change	sheep

A. Fill in the blank with the plural form of the word in parentheses.

1. (brush) These are plastic _____.

2. (lunch) That cafe on the corner serves well-balanced _____.

3. (country) What _____ belong to the United Nations?

4. (bench) There are many iron _____ in the park.

5. (earring) These _____ came from Italy.

6. (calf) How many _____ are in that pen?

7. (piano) There are three _____ in the warehouse.

8. (fox) Did you see the _____ at the zoo?

9. (daisy) We bought Susan a bunch of _____.

10. (potato) Do you like baked _____?

11. (dish) Please help wash the _____.

12. (store) There are three _____ near my house.

B. Write the correct plural form for each singular noun.

1. booklet _____
2. tomato _____
3. truck _____
4. chef _____
5. branch _____
6. toddler _____
7. penny _____
8. potato _____
9. piece _____
10. door _____
11. island _____
12. country _____
13. house _____
14. garage _____
15. fish _____

16. watch _____
17. elf _____
18. desk _____
19. pan _____
20. sheep _____
21. garden _____
22. pony _____
23. solo _____
24. tree _____
25. light _____
26. church _____
27. city _____
28. spoonful _____
29. vacation _____
30. home _____

C. Rewrite the sentences, changing each underlined singular noun to a plural noun.

1. Put the apple and orange in the box.

   _____

2. Jan wrote five letter to her friend.

   _____

3. Those building each have four elevator.

   _____

4. Our family drove many mile to get to the lake.

   _____

5. The top of those car were damaged in the storm.

   _____

6. My aunt and uncle attended the family reunion.

   _____

28 LESSON

Possessive Nouns

- A **possessive noun** shows possession of the noun that follows.
- Form the possessive of most singular nouns by adding an apostrophe (') and -s.
  EXAMPLES: the boy's hat   Mr. Thomas's car
- Form the possessive of a plural noun ending in -s by adding only an apostrophe.
  EXAMPLES: the Smiths' home   girls' bikes   sisters' names
- Form the possessive of a plural noun that does not end in -s by adding an apostrophe and -s.
  EXAMPLES: children's classes   men's books

A. Write the possessive form of each noun.

1. girl _____girl's_____
2. child _____
3. women _____
4. children _____
5. John _____

6. baby _____
7. boys _____
8. teacher _____
9. Dr. Ray _____
10. ladies _____

11. brother _____
12. soldier _____
13. men _____
14. aunt _____
15. Ms. Jones _____

B. Rewrite each phrase using a possessive noun.

1. the cap belonging to Jim _____Jim's cap_____

2. the wrench that belongs to Kathy _____

3. the smile of the baby _____

4. the car that my friend owns _____

5. the new shoes that belong to Kim _____

6. the collar of the dog _____

7. the golf clubs that Frank owns _____

8. the shoes that belong to the runners _____

9. the friends of our parents _____

10. the opinion of the editor _____

11. the lunches of the children _____

12. the coat belonging to Kyle _____

13. the assignment of the teacher _____

Appositives

LESSON 29

- An **appositive** is a noun that identifies or explains the noun or pronoun it follows.
    - EXAMPLE: My dog, **Fido,** won a medal.
- An **appositive phrase** consists of an appositive and its modifiers.
    - EXAMPLE: My book, **a novel about the Civil War,** is one of the best I've read.
- Use **commas** to set off an appositive or an appositive phrase that is not essential to the meaning of the sentence.
    - EXAMPLE: John Gray, my uncle, owns that home.
- Don't use commas if the appositive is essential to the meaning of the sentence.
    - EXAMPLES: My brother Kevin arrived late. My other brother Charlie arrived early.

A. Underline the appositive or appositive phrase, and circle the noun that it identifies.

1. Banff, the large Canadian national park, is my favorite place to visit.

2. The painter Vincent Van Gogh cut off part of his ear.

3. The White House, home of the President of the United States, is open to the public for tours.

4. Uncle Marco, my mother's brother, is an engineer.

5. Earth, the only inhabited planet in our solar system, is home to a diverse population of plants and animals.

6. The scorpion, a native of the southwestern part of North America, has a poisonous sting.

7. Emily's prize Persian cat Amelia won first prize at the cat show.

8. Judge Andropov, the presiding judge, sentenced the criminal to prison.

9. Paula's friend from Florida, Luisa, watched a space shuttle launch.

B. Complete each sentence with an appropriate appositive.

1. My friend _____ bought a new bike.

2. The bike, _____, is fast and sleek.

3. Joe and his friend _____ plan to ride their bikes together.

4. They will ride to Pease Park, _____, on Saturday.

5. They plan to meet Anne, _____, on the bike path.

6. After bicycling, they will see a movie, _____.

7. Our friend _____ might come with us.

8. We will get a snack, _____, to eat during the movie.

9. My favorite actor, _____, might be in the movie.

Unit 3, Grammar and Usage

30 Verbs

LESSON

■ A **verb** is a word that expresses action, being, or state of being.
  EXAMPLES: Leo **traveled** to Europe. Maura **is** an accountant.
■ A verb has four principal parts: **present, present participle, past,** and **past participle.**
■ For regular verbs, form the present participle by adding -ing to the present. Use a form of the helping verb be with the present participle.
■ Form the past and past participle by adding -ed to the present. Use a form of the helping verb have with the past participle.
  EXAMPLES:

Present	Present Participle	Past	Past Participle
listen	(is) listening	listened	(have, had, has) listened
help	(is) helping	helped	(have, had, has) helped
change	(is) changing	changed	(have, had, has) changed

■ Irregular verbs form their past and past participle in other ways. A dictionary shows the principal parts of these verbs.

■ **Write the present participle, past, and past participle for each verb.**

PRESENT	PRESENT PARTICIPLE	PAST	PAST PARTICIPLE
1. scatter	(is) scattering	scattered	(have, had, has) scattered
2. express			
3. paint			
4. call			
5. cook			
6. observe			
7. look			
8. walk			
9. ramble			
10. shout			
11. notice			
12. order			
13. gaze			
14. borrow			
15. start			
16. work			

31
LESSON

Verb Phrases

> ■ Some sentences contain a **verb phrase.** A verb phrase consists of a
> **main verb** and one or more other verbs.
> EXAMPLES: The women **are singing.** Where **have** you **been?**

■ **Underline the verb or verb phrase in each sentence.**

1. The first American schools were held in homes.

2. Who invented the jet engine?

3. *The New England Primer* was the earliest United States textbook.

4. John Philip Sousa was a bandmaster and composer.

5. Who built the first motorcycle?

6. My friends will arrive on Saturday afternoon.

7. What was the final score?

8. Ryan has made this unusual birdhouse.

9. The waves covered the beach with many shells.

10. I have ridden on a motor scooter.

11. The artist is molding clay.

12. Beverly and her friends spent last summer in the mountains.

13. The names of the new employees are posted by the supervisor.

14. Paul has found a new hat.

15. She is going to the store.

16. We have trimmed the hedges.

17. The United States exports many kinds of food.

18. My friend is reading a book about World War I.

19. Jane Addams helped many foreign-born people in Chicago, Illinois.

20. Oil was discovered in many parts of North America.

21. Jenny Lind was called the Swedish Nightingale.

22. We are planning a car trip to Miami, Florida.

23. That dog has howled for two hours.

24. Our guests have arrived.

25. I have written letters to several companies.

26. I can name two important cities in that country.

27. The hummingbird received its name because of the sound of its wings.

28. Jan's poem was printed in the newspaper.

29. Charles and Adam are working at the hamburger stand.

30. This table was painted recently.

32 LESSON

Verb Tenses

- The **tense** of a verb tells the time of the action or being. There are three simple tenses—present, past, and future.
- **Present tense** tells about what is happening now.
  EXAMPLES: Conrad **is** busy. Conrad **studies** hard.
- **Past tense** tells about something that happened before.
  EXAMPLE: Conrad **was** sick yesterday.
- **Future tense** tells about something that will happen. The auxiliary verbs will and shall are used in future tense.
  EXAMPLES: Conrad **will take** the test tomorrow. I **shall keep** my word.

A. Complete each sentence by writing a verb in the tense shown in parentheses.

1. (future)   Hilary _____ tomorrow.

2. (future)   Joe _____ her up at the airport.

3. (past)   We _____ the house yesterday.

4. (past)   Carl _____ reservations for tomorrow night.

5. (present)   Hilary _____ my friend.

6. (future)   We _____ on a sightseeing tour.

7. (present)   I _____ very excited about Hilary's visit.

8. (past)   Margaret _____ Toby last week.

B. Write present, past, or future for the tense of each underlined verb.

1. Classes will end next month.   _____

2. We studied hard yesterday.   _____

3. Final exams will start soon.   _____

4. I review every evening.   _____

5. This method worked at midterm.   _____

6. I got A's on my tests then.   _____

7. Marty studies with me.   _____

8. We will study every evening this week.   _____

9. I hardly studied last year.   _____

10. My grades showed it, too.   _____

Present Perfect and Past Perfect Tenses

- The **perfect tenses** express action that happened before another time or event.
- The **present perfect** tense tells about something that happened at an indefinite time in the past. The present perfect tense consists of <u>has</u> or <u>have</u> + the past participle.
  - EXAMPLES: I **have eaten** already. He **has eaten,** too.
- The **past perfect** tense tells about something that happened before something else in the past. The past perfect tense consists of <u>had</u> + the past participle.
  - EXAMPLE: I already **had eaten** when they arrived.

A. Write <u>present perfect</u> and <u>past perfect</u> for the tense of the underlined verbs.

_____ **1.** Mei <u>had completed</u> high school in June.

_____ **2.** She <u>had gone</u> to college in Memphis before coming here.

_____ **3.** Mei <u>has decided</u> that she likes her new college.

_____ **4.** She <u>had been worried</u> that she wouldn't fit in.

_____ **5.** Mei <u>has lived</u> in her house for eight months.

_____ **6.** We <u>have tried</u> to make Mei feel welcome.

_____ **7.** She <u>has told</u> us a great deal about Memphis.

_____ **8.** We <u>had known</u> Memphis was an important city.

_____ **9.** However, Mei <u>has described</u> things we never knew!

_____ **10.** We <u>have decided</u> that we would like to visit Tennessee some day.

B. Complete each sentence with <u>have</u>, <u>has</u>, or <u>had</u> to form the verb tense indicated in parentheses.

1. (present perfect)   The pitcher _____ left the mound.

2. (present perfect)   The coach and catcher _____ talked to him.

3. (past perfect)   The coach _____ warned him to be careful.

4. (present perfect)   Jason _____ taken his place on the mound.

5. (past perfect)   Jason _____ pitched ten games by the end of last season.

6. (present perfect)   Jason _____ pitched very well.

7. (past perfect)   The team _____ won every game last week.

34
LESSON

Using *Is/Are* and *Was/Were*

- Use <u>is</u> with a singular subject.
  EXAMPLE: Tasha **is** the winner.
- Use <u>are</u> with a plural subject.
  EXAMPLE: The boys **are** walking home.
- Always use <u>are</u> with the pronoun <u>you</u>.
  EXAMPLE: <u>You</u> **are** absolutely right!

A. Underline the correct verb to complete each sentence.

1. (Is, Are) this tool ready to be cleaned?

2. They (is, are) making peanut brittle.

3. Bill (is, are) the chairperson this week.

4. Where (is, are) my gloves?

5. This tomato (is, are) too ripe.

6. Ryan, (is, are) these your books?

7. Daniel, (is, are) the sandwiches ready?

8. (Is, Are) you going to sing your solo this morning?

9. This newspaper (is, are) the early edition.

10. Carol asked if you (is, are) still coming to the game.

- Use <u>was</u> with a singular subject to tell about the past.
  EXAMPLE: I **was** there yesterday.
- Use <u>were</u> with a plural subject to tell about the past.
  EXAMPLE: Kevin and Ray **were** not home.
- Always use <u>were</u> with the pronoun <u>you</u>.
  EXAMPLE: <u>You</u> **were** only a few minutes late.

B. Underline the correct verb to complete each sentence.

1. Amy and Crystal (was, were) disappointed because they could not go.

2. Our seats (was, were) near the stage.

3. Taro, Bill, and Luis (was, were) assigned to the first team.

4. These pencils (was, were) made by a company in Chicago.

5. There (was, were) only one carton of milk in the refrigerator.

6. Who (was, were) that person on the corner?

7. She (was, were) at my house this morning.

8. You (was, were) the best swimmer in the contest.

9. Those tomatoes (was, were) delicious!

10. He (was, were) late for work today.

35

LESSON

Past Tenses of *See*, *Go*, and *Begin*

- Never use a helping verb with <u>saw</u>, <u>went</u>, and <u>began</u>.
- Always use a helping verb with <u>seen</u>, <u>gone</u>, and <u>begun</u>.

A. Underline the correct verb.

1. The last person we (saw, seen) in the park was Eric.

2. Who has (went, gone) for the ice?

3. Carla and Yoko (began, begun) to fix the flat tire.

4. Charles (went, gone) to the supermarket for some lettuce.

5. Our summer vacation has (began, begun).

6. They had (saw, seen) a shooting star.

7. Hasn't she (went, gone) to the airport?

8. Yes, we (saw, seen) the concert poster.

9. Alice, have you ever (saw, seen) a penguin?

10. We never (went, gone) to hear the new mayor speak.

11. Olivia, why haven't you (began, begun) your work?

12. Mike (began, begun) to tell us about the accident.

13. Our guests have (went, gone).

14. It (began, begun) to snow early in the evening.

15. Work has finally (began, begun) on the new stadium.

16. We (saw, seen) Pikes Peak last summer.

17. My three sisters (went, gone) to Toronto, Ontario.

18. Have you (saw, seen) the waves pounding the huge boulders?

19. We (went, gone) to hear the symphony last night.

20. They (began, begun) their program with music by Mozart.

21. The program (began, begun) on time.

B. Write a sentence using each verb below.

1. saw _____

2. seen _____

3. gone _____

4. went _____

5. began _____

6. begun _____

36 LESSON

Past Tenses of *Freeze, Choose, Speak,* and *Break*

- Never use a helping verb with: <u>froze</u> <u>chose</u> <u>spoke</u> <u>broke</u>
- Always use a helping verb with: <u>frozen</u> <u>chosen</u> <u>spoken</u> <u>broken</u>

A. Underline the correct verb form to complete each sentence.

1. Haven't those candidates (spoke, spoken) yet?

2. Has the dessert (froze, frozen) in the molds?

3. I (broke, broken) the handle of the hammer.

4. Have you (spoke, spoken) to your friends about the meeting?

5. Hadn't the coach (chose, chosen) the best players today?

6. The dog has (broke, broken) the toy.

7. Has Anna (spoke, spoken) to you about going with us?

8. We (froze, frozen) the ice for our picnic.

9. I believe you (chose, chosen) the right clothes.

10. Dave, haven't you (broke, broken) your bat?

11. Mr. Mann (spoke, spoken) first.

12. Anthony (froze, frozen) the fruit salad for our picnic.

13. You didn't tell me he had (broke, broken) his arm.

14. The men on the team (chose, chosen) their plays carefully.

15. Ms. Ramirez (spoke, spoken) first.

16. Has the river (froze, frozen) yet?

B. Write the correct past tense form of the verb in parentheses to complete each sentence.

1. (freeze) We could not tell if the ice had _____ overnight.

2. (break) The chain on Ann's bicycle had _____ while she rode.

3. (choose) Carol had _____ to be in the play.

4. (speak) No one _____ while the band played.

5. (choose) Tom has _____ to take both tests today.

6. (choose) Jim _____ not to take the test early.

7. (break) No one knew who had _____ the window.

8. (speak) Carol _____ her lines loudly and clearly.

9. (freeze) It was so cold that everything had _____.

10. (speak) The librarian wanted to know who had _____ so loudly.

37 LESSON

Come, Ring, Drink, Know, and Throw

- Never use a helping verb with came, rang, drank, knew, and threw.
- Always use a helping verb with come, rung, drunk, known, and thrown.

A. Underline the correct verb.

1. The tired horse (drank, drunk) from the cool stream.

2. The church bell has not (rang, rung) today.

3. I haven't (drank, drunk) my hot chocolate.

4. We (knew, known) that it was time to go.

5. Have you (threw, thrown) the garbage out?

6. Haven't the movers (came, come) for our furniture?

7. We (rang, rung) the fire alarm five minutes ago.

8. Haven't you (know, known) him for a long time?

9. I (threw, thrown) the ball to James.

10. My friends from London, England, (came, come) this afternoon.

11. Why haven't you (drank, drunk) your juice?

12. I always (came, come) to work in my wheelchair now.

13. I (knew, known) Pat when she was just a child.

14. Have you (threw, thrown) away last week's newspaper?

15. We have (came, come) to tell you something.

16. If you already (rang, rung) the bell, then you might try knocking.

17. Tony thinks he (drank, drunk) something that made him ill.

B. Write a sentence using each verb below.

1. came _____

2. come _____

3. rang _____

4. rung _____

5. threw _____

6. thrown _____

7. drank _____

8. drunk _____

9. knew _____

 **38**
LESSON

Past Tenses of *Give, Take,* and *Write*

- Never use a helping verb with <u>gave</u>, <u>took</u>, and <u>wrote</u>.
- Always use a helping verb with <u>given</u>, <u>taken</u>, and <u>written</u>.

A. Underline the correct verb.

1. It (took, taken) the mechanic only a few minutes to change the tire.

2. Has anyone (took, taken) my note pad?

3. Who (wrote, written) the best letter?

4. I have (wrote, written) a thank-you note.

5. Tell me who (gave, given) you that address.

6. Have you (gave, given) the dog its food?

7. Bill hadn't (wrote, written) this poem.

8. Have you finally (wrote, written) for the tickets?

9. Emilio had (gave, given) the lecture on boat safety yesterday at the Y.M.C.A.

10. Alicia and I (wrote, written) a letter to the editor.

11. Haven't you (took, taken) your seat yet?

12. We had our picture (took, taken) yesterday.

13. Who (gave, given) you these old magazines?

14. The workers (took, taken) all their equipment with them.

15. A friend had (gave, given) us the furniture.

16. Leslie had (wrote, written) the letter over three weeks ago.

17. Who (took, taken) the most photographs on the trip?

18. The doctor (gave, given) me a tetanus shot after I cut my hand.

19. Has Brian (wrote, written) to Julia yet?

B. Write the correct past tense form of each verb in parentheses to complete the sentences.

1. (take) Amanda recently _____ her dog, Ralph, to the veterinarian.

2. (write) The doctor had _____ to say that Ralph needed his annual shots.

3. (give) An assistant _____ Ralph a dog biscuit as soon as he arrived.

4. (give) That way Ralph was _____ something that would distract him.

5. (take) Before Ralph knew it, the doctor had _____ a sample of his blood.

6. (take) It only _____ a minute to give Ralph his shots.

7. (give) The doctor _____ Ralph a pat on the head.

8. (take) "You have _____ very good care of Ralph," he said.

Unit 3, Grammar and Usage

39
LESSON

Eat, Fall, Draw, Drive, and Run

■ Never use a helping verb with <u>ate</u>, <u>fell</u>, <u>drew</u>, <u>drove</u>, and <u>ran</u>.
■ Always use a helping verb with <u>eaten</u>, <u>fallen</u>, <u>drawn</u>, <u>driven</u>, and <u>run</u>.

A. Underline the correct verb.

1. Taro, have you (drew, drawn) your diagram?

2. When we had (drove, driven) for two hours, we (began, begun) to feel hungry.

3. All of our pears have (fell, fallen) from the tree.

4. After we had (ate, eaten) our dinner, we (ran, run) around the lake.

5. A great architect (drew, drawn) the plans for our civic center.

6. We had just (ran, run) into the house when we saw our friends.

7. Hadn't the building already (fell, fallen) when you (ran, run) around the corner?

8. Those heavy curtains in the theater have (fell, fallen) down.

9. Last week we (drove, driven) to the lake for a vacation.

10. I have just (ate, eaten) a delicious slice of pizza.

11. I (ate, eaten) my breakfast before six o'clock this morning.

12. All of the leaves have (fell, fallen) from the elm trees.

13. When was the last time you (ran, run) a mile?

B. Write the correct past tense form of each verb in parentheses to complete the sentences.

1. (drive) Last weekend we _____ to the lake for a picnic.

2. (draw) Since Jenna knew several shortcuts, she _____ a detailed map for us.

3. (fall) She mentioned that during a recent summer storm, debris had _____ on many of the roads.

4. (fall) She warned us that a large tree _____ on one of the main roads.

5. (drive) Jenna claimed that she had never _____ under such dangerous circumstances.

6. (run) "I almost _____ right into that tree in the dark!" Jenna said.

7. (eat) In order to avoid traveling at night, we _____ our dinner after we got home from the lake.

8. (eat) We had _____ so much during our picnic that none of us minded waiting!

9. (draw) Once home, we all agreed that Jenna had _____ a great map for us.

10. (run) We made the trip in record time, and we hadn't _____ over any trees in the process!

---

54   Unit 3, Grammar and Usage

40 Forms of *Do*

LESSON

- Never use a helping verb with <u>did</u>.
  EXAMPLE: Anne **did** a great job on her test.
- Always use a helping verb with <u>done</u>.
  EXAMPLE: Hallie **had** also **done** a great job.
- <u>Doesn't</u> is the contraction of <u>does not</u>. Use it with singular nouns and the pronouns <u>he</u>, <u>she</u>, and <u>it</u>.
  EXAMPLES: Rachel **doesn't** want to go. It **doesn't** seem right.
- <u>Don't</u> is the contraction of <u>do not</u>. Use it with plural nouns and with the pronouns <u>I</u>, <u>you</u>, <u>we</u>, and <u>they</u>.
  EXAMPLES: Mr. and Mrs. Ricci **don't** live there. You **don't** have your purse.

A. Underline the correct verb.

1. Why (doesn't, don't) Lois have the car keys?

2. Show me the way you (did, done) it.

3. Have the three of you (did, done) most of the work?

4. Why (doesn't, don't) she cash a check today?

5. Please show me what damage the storm (did, done).

6. (Doesn't, Don't) the workers on the morning shift do a fine job?

7. Have the new owners of our building (did, done) anything about the plumbing?

8. (Doesn't, Don't) those apples look overly ripe?

9. Chris (doesn't, don't) want to do the spring cleaning this week.

10. The gloves and the hat (doesn't, don't) match.

11. Carolyn, have you (did, done) your homework today?

12. Who (did, done) this fine job of painting?

13. (Doesn't, Don't) the tile in our new kitchen look nice?

14. (Doesn't, Don't) that dog stay in a fenced yard?

15. He has (did, done) me a great favor.

16. I will help if he (doesn't, don't).

B. Write one sentence using <u>did</u> and one sentence using <u>done</u>.

1. _____

2. _____

C. Write one sentence using <u>doesn't</u> and one sentence using <u>don't</u>.

1. _____

2. _____

41 LESSON

Mood

> ■ **Mood** is a form of the verb that shows the manner of doing or being. There are three types of moods: **indicative, subjunctive,** and **imperative.**
> ■ **Indicative mood** states a fact or asks a question.
>   EXAMPLES: Ben **came** Friday. How many **went** to the meeting?
> ■ **Subjunctive mood** can indicate a wish or a contrary-to-fact condition. Use <u>were</u> to express the subjunctive.
>   EXAMPLE: I would help you, if I **were** able. (I am not able.)
> ■ **Imperative mood** expresses a command or a request.
>   EXAMPLES: **Ask** no more questions. Let's **start** immediately.

■ **Give the mood of each underlined word.**

1. <u>Come</u> here at once. _____

2. I <u>did</u> not <u>see</u> Carolyn. _____

3. If I <u>were</u> not so tired, I would go to a movie. _____

4. <u>Call</u> for him at once. _____

5. Where <u>has</u> Brittany <u>moved</u>? _____

6. Who <u>invented</u> the sewing machine? _____

7. Juanita <u>came</u> Saturday. _____

8. Paul wishes it <u>were</u> true. _____

9. <u>Come</u> here, Jennifer. _____

10. I wish it <u>were</u> summer. _____

11. <u>Be</u> home early. _____

12. <u>Ring</u> the bell immediately. _____

13. The members of the band <u>sold</u> birthday calendars. _____

14. If I <u>were</u> you, I'd stop that. _____

15. Zachary <u>likes</u> my new sweater. _____

16. My friends <u>painted</u> the entire house. _____

17. If this <u>were</u> a sunny day, I would go with you. _____

18. <u>Tell</u> us where you went. _____

19. He greeted me as though I <u>were</u> a stranger. _____

42

LESSON

Transitive and Intransitive Verbs

- There are two kinds of action verbs: **transitive** and **intransitive**.
- A transitive verb has a direct object.
  D.O.
  EXAMPLE: Jeffrey **painted** the house.
- An intransitive verb does not need an object to complete its meaning.
  EXAMPLES: The sun **rises** in the east. She **walks** quickly.

A. Underline the verb in each sentence. Then write T for transitive or I for intransitive.

_____ **1.** Kristina joined the health club in March.

_____ **2.** She wanted the exercise to help her stay healthy.

_____ **3.** Kristina exercised every day after work.

_____ **4.** She became friends with Nancy.

_____ **5.** They worked out together.

_____ **6.** Nancy preferred the treadmill.

_____ **7.** Kristina liked aerobics and running.

_____ **8.** Sometimes they switched activities.

_____ **9.** Nancy took an aerobics class.

_____ **10.** Kristina used the treadmill.

_____ **11.** Occasionally they swam in the pool.

_____ **12.** Nancy was the better swimmer.

_____ **13.** But Kristina had more fun.

_____ **14.** She just splashed around in the water.

B. Underline the transitive verb, and circle the direct object in each sentence.

1. Carlos walked Tiny every day.

2. Tiny usually pulled Carlos along.

3. Carlos washed Tiny every other week.

4. Tiny loved water.

5. He splashed Carlos whenever he could.

6. Tiny also loved rawhide bones.

7. He chewed the bones until they were gone.

8. Carlos found Tiny when Tiny was just a puppy.

Active and Passive Voice

LESSON 43

- **Voice** refers to the relation of a subject to its verb.
- In the **active voice,** the subject acts.
  - EXAMPLE: **I painted** the house.
- In the **passive voice,** the subject receives the action.
  - EXAMPLE: The house **was painted** by me.
- Only transitive verbs are used in the passive voice.

A. Write <u>A</u> if the sentence is in the active voice and <u>P</u> if it is in the passive voice.

_____ 1. Marty applied for a job in a grocery store.

_____ 2. He needs money for gas and car repairs.

_____ 3. He will handle the cash register.

_____ 4. Marty will also stock the shelves.

_____ 5. The application was turned in last week.

_____ 6. The store's manager reads every application.

_____ 7. Then the applicants are interviewed.

_____ 8. Marty was interviewed on Monday.

_____ 9. The manager was impressed by Marty.

_____ 10. He will give Marty the job.

B. Rewrite each sentence in the active voice.

1. Kate was given a job babysitting by the McNeils.

   _____

2. The children will be watched by her every day.

   _____

3. Kate will be driven to their house by her friend.

   _____

C. Rewrite each sentence in the passive voice.

1. Trina plays the drums in the band.

   _____

2. She chose the drums because her father played drums.

   _____

3. Trina won an award for her playing.

   _____

44

LESSON

Gerunds

■ A **gerund** is the present participle of a verb form ending in -ing that is used as a noun.
■ A gerund may be the subject, direct object, or object of a preposition.
  EXAMPLES: **Exercising** is vital to good health. (subject)
  Tanya enjoys **exercising**. (direct object)
  I have thought of **exercising**. (object of preposition)

■ **Underline each gerund.**

1. We enjoy living on the farm.

2. Airplanes are used in fighting forest fires.

3. Landing an airplane requires skill.

4. Climbing Pikes Peak is quite an experience.

5. The moaning of the wind through the pines lulled me to sleep.

6. The dog's barking awakened everyone in the house.

7. Keeping his temper is difficult for John.

8. Sue objected to our hanging the picture in this room.

9. Laughing aloud is encouraged by the comedian.

10. Being treasurer of this club is a responsibility.

11. Making a speech makes me nervous.

12. Winning this game will place our soccer team first in the league.

13. It was my first attempt at pitching horseshoes.

14. Rapid eating will make digestion difficult.

15. Playing golf is a favorite pastime in many countries.

16. Planning a party requires much thought.

17. We have completed our packing for the trip to the mountains.

18. The howling of the dogs disturbed our sleep.

19. I am tired of doing this work.

20. We are fond of living here.

21. Native Americans once spent much time planting, hunting, and fishing.

22. Neat writing is important in school.

23. I enjoy skating on this pond.

24. Jason taught us the rules of boating.

25. Pressing the wrong button can be very dangerous.

26. Airplanes are used in the mapping of large areas.

27. Swimming in this lake is my favorite sport.

28. I enjoy driving a car.

45 Infinitives

- **Underline each infinitive.**

1. I want <u>to go</u> home before it gets any colder.

2. We went to see the play while Emilio was here.

3. I prepared the salad to serve for lunch.

4. To shoot firecrackers in the city limits is against the law in some places.

5. I like to walk in the country.

6. They were taught to stand, to sit, to walk, and to dance gracefully.

7. Gradually people learned to use fire and to make tools.

8. I need to get a new coat.

9. We plan to make the trip in four hours.

10. Carol, are you too tired to clean the kitchen?

11. Jack, try to be on time in the morning.

12. Anthony plans to travel in Canada during August.

13. Who taught you to play golf?

14. We were taught to rise early.

15. We were hoping to see you at the reunion.

16. Pay one fee to enter the amusement park.

17. Jennifer, I forgot to mail your package.

18. To cook this turkey will require several hours.

19. The children ran to meet their friend.

20. We are learning to speak Spanish.

21. We are planning to exhibit our artwork next week.

22. To succeed as an artist was Rick's dream.

23. We went to see the parade.

24. We are ready to eat.

25. It was easy to see the reason for that actor's popularity.

26. The only way to have a friend is to be one.

27. Madame Curie was the only woman to receive the Nobel Prize a second time.

28. To score the most points is the object of the game.

29. We need to go grocery shopping.

30. Do you want to paint the fence on Saturday?

46 Participles

LESSON

- A **present** or **past participle** is a verb form that may be used as an adjective.

  EXAMPLES: A **dripping** faucet can be a nuisance. **Wilted** flowers were removed from the vase.

- **Underline each participle.**

1. We saw a <u>running</u> deer in the forest.

2. The chart showing sales figures is very helpful.

3. The scampering cat ran to the nearest tree.

4. A team of deep-sea divers discovered the hidden treasure.

5. We saw the thunderstorm advancing across the plains.

6. Biting insects hovered over our campsite at night.

7. His foot, struck by the falling timbers, was injured.

8. The whispering pines filled the air with their fresh scent.

9. People preparing for a career in aviation should master mathematics.

10. We drove slowly, enjoying every minute of the drive.

11. Onions are among the largest vegetable crops produced in the United States.

12. The truck, burdened with its load, traveled slowly over the rough road.

13. Jan, thinking about her new job, was very happy.

14. Several passengers injured in the wreck were brought to the local hospital.

15. That expanding city will soon be the largest one in the state.

16. The fire, fanned by the high winds, threatened the entire area.

17. The rude person, shoving others aside, went to see the manager.

18. The lake, frozen solidly, looked like a huge mirror.

19. The man playing the trombone is my brother.

20. The cleaned apartment was ready for new tenants.

21. Teasing children ran at Rip Van Winkle's heels.

22. Balloons lifting weather instruments are released daily by many weather stations.

23. The chirping bird flew from tree to tree.

24. The surviving pilot described the accident.

25. The dedicated artist worked patiently.

26. Homing pigeons were used in the experiment.

27. The whistling youngster skipped happily down the road.

28. Ironed shirts were stacked neatly at the cleaners.

29. Those standing near the fence should form a second line.

30. The child ran to his loving father, who comforted him.

47 LESSON

Using *May/Can* and *Teach/Learn*

> - Use <u>may</u> to ask for permission.
>   EXAMPLE: **May** I go with you?
> - Use <u>can</u> to express the ability to do something.
>   EXAMPLE: James **can** swim well.

A. Complete each sentence with <u>may</u> or <u>can</u>.

1. Adam, _____ you whistle?

2. His dog _____ do three difficult tricks.

3. Miss Nance, _____ I leave work early?

4. I _____ see the airplane in the distance.

5. Chris, _____ you tie a good knot?

6. Carlos, _____ I drive your car?

7. You _____ see the mountains from here.

8. My friend _____ drive us home.

9. The Garcias _____ speak three languages.

10. _____ I examine those new books?

> - Teach means "to give instruction."
>   EXAMPLE: I'll **teach** you how to shoot free throws.
> - Learn means "to acquire knowledge."
>   EXAMPLE: When did you **learn** to speak Spanish?

B. Complete each sentence with <u>teach</u> or <u>learn</u>.

1. I think he will _____ me quickly.

2. I will _____ to recite that poem.

3. Did Jamie _____ you to build a fire?

4. The women are going to _____ to use the new machines.

5. Will you _____ me to play tennis?

6. My brother is going to _____ Billy to skate.

7. Would you like to _____ the rules of the game to them?

8. No one can _____ you if you do not try to _____.

48 LESSON

Using *Sit/Set* and *Lay/Lie*

- Sit means "to take a resting position." Its principal parts are sit, sitting, and sat.
  EXAMPLES: Please **sit** here. He **sat** beside her.
- Set means "to place." Its principal parts are set, setting, and set.
  EXAMPLES: Will you please **set** this dish on the table?
  She **set** the table for dinner last night.

A. Underline the correct verb.

1. Please (sit, set) down, Kathleen.

2. Where should we (sit, set) the television?

3. Where do you (sit, set)?

4. Pamela, please (sit, set) those plants out this afternoon.

5. (Sit, Set) the basket of groceries on the patio.

6. José usually (sits, sets) on this side of the table.

7. Please come and (sit, set) your books down on that desk.

8. Have you ever (sat, set) by this window?

9. Does he (sit, set) in this seat?

10. Why don't you (sit, set) over here?

- Lie means "to recline" or "to occupy a certain space." Its principal parts are lie, lying, lay, and lain.
  EXAMPLES: Why don't you **lie** down for a while?
  He **has lain** in the hammock all afternoon.
- Lay means "to place." Its principal parts are lay, laying, and laid.
  EXAMPLES: The men **are laying** new carpeting in the house.
  Who **laid** the wet towel on the table?

B. Underline the correct verb.

1. Where did you (lie, lay) your gloves, Beth?

2. (Lie, Lay) down, Spot.

3. He always (lies, lays) down to rest when he is very tired.

4. Where have you (lain, laid) the evening paper?

5. Please (lie, lay) this box on the desk.

6. Do not (lie, lay) on that dusty hay.

7. (Lay, Lie) the papers on top of the desk.

8. I (laid, lain) the shovel on that pile of dirt.

9. I need to (lie, lay) down to rest.

10. She has (laid, lain) on the sofa all morning.

49 Pronouns

LESSON

- A **pronoun** is a word used in place of a noun.
- A **personal pronoun** is chosen based on the way it is used in the sentence.
  A **subject pronoun** is used in the subject of a sentence and after a linking verb.
  EXAMPLES: **He** is a chemist. The chemist is **he**.
  An **object pronoun** is used after an action verb or a preposition.
  EXAMPLES: Jan gave **me** the gift. Jan gave the gift to **me**.
  A **possessive pronoun** is used to show ownership of something.
  EXAMPLES: The new car is **ours**. That is **our** car.

■ **Underline each pronoun.**

1. Brian, do you have my ticket to the play?

2. Just between you and me, I want to go with them.

3. Carol, will you help me carry our trunk?

4. May I go with you?

5. We saw him standing in line to go to a movie.

6. Just be sure to find Carol and me.

7. We will be ready when they come for us.

8. She sent this box of frozen steaks to Andrea and me.

9. She asked you and me to be on her bowling team.

10. We saw them go into the building on the corner.

11. Last week we sent flowers to our sick friend.

12. He must choose their dinner.

13. She is my English instructor.

14. They have never invited us to go with them.

15. The first-place winner is she.

16. Can he compete against you?

17. She made the dinner for us.

18. Liz and I are going on vacation in June.

19. Where is your umbrella?

20. Sharon gave me a book to read.

21. Do you know where our cottage is?

22. If I lend you my car, will you take care of it?

23. I gave him my word that we would visit her.

24. When they saw us fishing, Bob and Diane changed their clothes.

25. Your toes are peeking through your socks.

26. Marie showed us how to fasten her bike to our car.

Demonstrative and Indefinite Pronouns

> - A **demonstrative pronoun** is used to point out a specific person or thing.
> - <u>This</u> and <u>that</u> are used in place of singular nouns. <u>This</u> refers to a person or thing nearby, and <u>that</u> refers to a person or thing farther away.
>   EXAMPLES: **This** is mine. **That** is the right one.
> - <u>These</u> and <u>those</u> are used in place of plural nouns. <u>These</u> points to persons or things nearby, and <u>those</u> points to persons or things farther away.
>   EXAMPLES: **These** are the best ones. **Those** don't look ripe.

A. Underline each demonstrative pronoun.

1. Those are the books I lost.

2. That is where Anne lives.

3. I'm not sure these are my scissors.

4. This is my pen; that is Pam's book.

5. I think those are interesting books.

6. Is that your first mistake?

7. This is Gretchen's timecard.

8. Give these to your friend.

9. These are Stephanie's shoes.

10. Please don't mention this.

11. I think those are just rumors.

12. Will this be our last chance?

13. Dave, those are your messages.

14. These are large peaches.

15. Sorry, that was my last piece.

16. Who told you that?

> - An **indefinite pronoun** does not refer to a specific person or thing.
>   EXAMPLE: **Many** are called, but **few** are chosen.
> - The indefinite pronouns <u>anybody</u>, <u>anyone</u>, <u>anything</u>, <u>each</u>, <u>everyone</u>, <u>everybody</u>, <u>everything</u>, <u>nobody</u>, <u>no one</u>, <u>nothing</u>, <u>one</u>, <u>somebody</u>, <u>someone</u>, and <u>something</u> are singular. They take singular verbs.
>   EXAMPLE: **Everyone is** ready.
> - The indefinite pronouns <u>both</u>, <u>few</u>, <u>many</u>, <u>several</u>, and <u>some</u> are plural. They take plural verbs.
>   EXAMPLE: **Several are** ready.

B. Underline each indefinite pronoun.

1. Both worked hard.

2. Let each help decorate.

3. Several have called about the job.

4. Unfortunately, some never learn.

5. Everyone was delighted at our party.

6. I think someone forgot this sweater.

7. Some asked for pens.

8. He thinks that each is right.

9. Has anyone seen my wallet?

10. Will someone wash the dishes?

11. Both of the singers are here.

12. One is absent.

13. Each must carry a bag.

14. Some always succeed.

15. Did someone leave this lunch?

16. Everybody is to be here early.

Antecedents

- An **antecedent** is the word to which a pronoun refers.
  EXAMPLE: **Stars** are lovely when **they** shine.
- A pronoun must agree with its antecedent in **gender (masculine, feminine,** or **neuter)** and **number (singular** or **plural).**
  EXAMPLES: **Susan** helped **her** friend. The **people** went in **their** cars.
- If the antecedent is an indefinite pronoun, it is correct to use a masculine pronoun. However, it is now common to use both a masculine and feminine pronoun.
  EXAMPLES: **Someone** lost **his** dog. **Someone** lost **his or her** dog.

- **Underline the correct pronoun, and circle its antecedent.**

1. (Everyone) should work hard at (their, <u>his or her</u>) job.

2. Each of the children willingly did (his or her, their) share of the camp duties.

3. Sophia gave me (her, their) coat to wear.

4. I took (my, our) friend to the ceremony.

5. All members were asked to bring (his or her, their) contributions today.

6. The women have had (her, their) vacation.

7. Someone has left (her or his, their) automobile across the driveway.

8. If each does (his or her, their) best, our chorus will win.

9. Would you tell Joanne that (her, his) soup is ready?

10. Every woman did (her, their) best to make the program a success.

11. Never judge anyone entirely by (his or her, their) looks.

12. Each student should do (his or her, their) own work.

13. I lost (my, our) favorite earring at the dance.

14. Each woman takes (her, their) own equipment on the camping trip.

15. Each one has a right to (his or her, their) own opinion in this matter.

16. (His, Her) sense of humor is what I like best about Joseph.

17. Some man has left (his, their) raincoat.

18. The two waiters dropped (his, their) trays when they bumped into each other.

19. Has each student received (his or her, their) report card?

20. Every person is expected to do (her or his, their) best.

21. We knew that every man at the meeting expressed (his, their) opinion.

22. Every woman furnishes (her, their) own transportation.

23. Jeff and Tom found (his, their) cabin in the dark.

24. Cliff brings his dog every time (he, she) visits.

25. The bird was in (their, its) nest.

26. Mark read (his, her) final essay for me.

Relative Pronouns

> ■ A **relative pronoun** is a pronoun that can introduce a subordinate clause. The relative pronouns are <u>who</u>, <u>whom</u>, <u>whose</u> (referring to persons); <u>which</u> (referring to things); and <u>that</u> (referring to persons or things).
>
> ■ A **subordinate clause**, when introduced by a relative pronoun, serves as an adjective. It modifies a word, or antecedent, in the main clause.
> EXAMPLES: Tom knows the author **whose** articles we read in class. The family for **whom** I work is from Canada. The movie **that** won the prize is playing.

■ **Underline each relative pronoun, and circle its antecedent.**

1. The (letter) <u>that</u> was published in our daily paper was very long.

2. It was Karen who sang the most difficult song.

3. Robert Burns, who wrote "My Heart's in the Highlands," was Scottish.

4. It was Sylvia who wanted Zach's address.

5. The shop that was filled with video games is going out of business.

6. My parents live in a New England farmhouse that was built many years ago.

7. This is the pearl that is so valuable.

8. The bridge, which is made of wood, was built two hundred years ago.

9. Did you see the animal that ran across the road?

10. Good roads have opened up many regions that were formerly impassable.

11. For our Thanksgiving dinner, we had a turkey that weighed twenty pounds.

12. This story, which was written by Eudora Welty, is most interesting.

13. Anna is a person whom you can trust.

14. We ate the delicious hamburgers that Andrew had prepared.

15. Food that is eaten in pleasant surroundings is usually digested easily.

16. This is the first painting that I did.

17. The sweater that you want is too expensive.

18. She is the one whom we watched at the track meet.

19. The only money that they spent was for food.

20. Your friend is one person who is inconsiderate.

21. A rare animal that lives in our city zoo was featured on the evening news.

22. Heather is one of the guests whom I invited.

23. Is this the file for which you've been searching?

24. Leonardo da Vinci is the artist whose work they most admire.

25. The science museum is an attraction that is visited by many tourists.

26. Charles Dickens is a writer whom I've read extensively.

Using *Who/Whom*

> - Use <u>who</u> as a subject pronoun. EXAMPLE: **Who** came to the party?
> - Use <u>whom</u> as an object pronoun. EXAMPLE: **Whom** did the nurse help?
> - By rearranging the sentence <u>The nurse did help **whom**?</u>, you can see that <u>whom</u> follows the verb and is the object of the verb. It can also be the object of a preposition. EXAMPLE: To **whom** did you wish to speak?

- **Complete each sentence with <u>Who</u> or <u>Whom</u>.**

1. _____Who_____ is that man?

2. _____ made the first moon landing?

3. _____ would you choose as the winner?

4. _____ is your best friend?

5. _____ gets the reward?

6. _____ will be staying with you this summer?

7. _____ did the instructor invite to speak to the class?

8. _____ did you see at the park?

9. _____ will you contact at headquarters?

10. _____ will you write about?

11. _____ is available to baby-sit for me on Saturday?

12. _____ did you drive to the store?

13. _____ would like to travel to Hawaii next summer?

14. _____ raced in the track meet?

15. _____ did they meet at the airport?

16. _____ are your three favorite authors?

17. _____ owns that new blue car?

18. _____ did you help last week?

19. _____ wrote that clever poem?

20. _____ will you ask to help you move?

21. _____ brought that salad?

54 LESSON

Adjectives

- An **adjective** is a word that modifies a noun or a pronoun.
  - EXAMPLE: He likes **chocolate** cookies.
- Adjectives usually tell **what kind, which one,** or **how many.**
  - EXAMPLES: **bright** penny, **these** oranges, **twelve** classmates
- A **proper adjective** is an adjective that is formed from a proper noun. It always begins with a capital letter.
  - EXAMPLES: **Asian** continent, **English** language
- The articles <u>a</u>, <u>an</u>, and <u>the</u> are called **limiting adjectives.**

A. Write three adjectives to describe each noun.

1. mountains _____   _____   _____

2. weather _____   _____   _____

3. journey _____   _____   _____

4. classroom _____   _____   _____

5. book _____   _____   _____

B. Underline each adjective.

1. This old chair is comfortable.

2. We have read a funny story recently.

3. This heavy traffic creates many dangerous situations.

4. The eager sailors collected odd souvenirs at every port.

5. The tired, thirsty soldiers marched on.

6. This is my favorite book.

7. The solitary guard walked along the lonely beach.

8. We sat in the sixth row.

9. These damp matches will not strike.

10. Dan made French toast for breakfast.

11. Will you light those candles, please?

12. A red bird chirped loudly in the tall tree.

13. The heavy elephant sat down slowly.

14. A tour bus stopped at the pirate's cove.

15. The gorgeous model wore Italian leather.

16. We ate fresh seafood on our vacation.

17. Do you like mashed or baked potatoes?

18. She served Chinese food for dinner.

---

55 Demonstrative Adjectives

LESSON

> - A **demonstrative adjective** is one that points out a specific person or thing.
> - This and that modify singular nouns. This points to a person or thing nearby, and that points to a person or thing farther away.
>   EXAMPLES: **This** movie is my favorite. **That** sign is difficult to see.
> - These and those modify plural nouns. These points to persons or things nearby and those points to persons or things farther away.
>   EXAMPLES: **These** ribbons are the most colorful.
>   **Those** towels need to be folded.
> - The word them is a pronoun. Never use it to describe a noun.

■ **Underline the correct demonstrative adjective.**

1. Move (those, them) plants inside since it may freeze tonight.

2. (These, That) box in front of me is too heavy to lift.

3. Who brought us (those, them) delicious cookies?

4. Look at (those, them) playful kittens.

5. (That, Those) kind of friend is appreciated.

6. (Those, Them) pictures are beautiful.

7. What are (those, them) sounds I hear?

8. Did you ever meet (those, them) people?

9. We have just developed (these, them) photographs.

10. Do you know any of (those, them) young people?

11. May we take some of (these, them) folders?

12. I have been looking over (these, them) magazines.

13. Do not eat too many of (those, them) peaches.

14. I do not like (this, these) kind of syrup.

15. (Those, Them) people should be served next.

16. Jimmy, please mail (these, them) letters.

17. Look at (those, them) posters I made!

18. (This, That) suburb is fifty miles away.

19. (These, Them) antique coins are valuable.

20. Look at (those, that) soccer players hustle!

21. José, may we see (these, them) photographs?

22. Please return (that, these) library books.

23. (These, Them) clothes need to be washed.

24. Please hand me (that, those) plates.

25. (Those, Them) cookies have nuts in them.

Comparing with Adjectives

LESSON 56

- An adjective has three degrees of comparison: **positive, comparative,** and **superlative.**
- The simple form of the adjective is called the **positive** degree.
    - EXAMPLE: Ian is **short.**
- When two people or things are being compared, the **comparative** degree is used.
    - EXAMPLE: Ian is **shorter** than Lee.
- When three or more people or things are being compared, the **superlative** degree is used.
    - EXAMPLE: Ian is the **shortest** person in the group.
- For all adjectives of one syllable and a few adjectives of two syllables, add -er to form the comparative degree, and -est to form the superlative degree.
    - EXAMPLE: smart—smarter—smartest
- For some adjectives of two syllables and all adjectives of three or more syllables, use more or less to form the comparative and most or least to form the superlative.
    - EXAMPLES: This test is **more** difficult than I expected. Carol is the **most** generous of all. Kate is **less** talkative than Tom. Mary is the **least** talkative of all.

- **Complete each sentence with the correct degree of comparison of the adjective given in parentheses. Some of the forms are irregular.**

1. (changeable) The weather seems _____ this year than last.

2. (faithful) I think the dog is the _____ of all animals.

3. (agreeable) Is James _____ than Sam?

4. (busy) Theresa is the _____ person in the office.

5. (long) Which is the _____ river, the Mississippi or the Amazon?

6. (lovely) I think the rose is the _____ of all flowers.

7. (fresh) Show me the _____ cookies in the store.

8. (high) Which of the two mountains is _____?

9. (enjoyable) Which is the _____, television or the movies?

10. (reckless) That person is the _____ driver in town.

11. (young) Of all the players, Maria is the _____.

12. (tall) Alberto is the _____ of the three men.

13. (difficult) Isn't the seventh problem _____ than the eighth?

14. (quiet) We have found the _____ spot in the park.

Adverbs

LESSON 57

- An **adverb** is a word that modifies a verb, an adjective, or another adverb.
    EXAMPLES: The rain poured **steadily**. His memories were **extremely** vivid. She responded **very** quickly.
- An adverb usually tells **how, when, where,** or **how often.**
- Many adverbs end in <u>-ly</u>.

A. Underline each adverb.

1. The person read slowly but clearly and expressively.

2. Adam, you are driving too recklessly.

3. The airplane started moving slowly but quickly gained speed.

4. I spoke too harshly to my friends.

5. How did all of you get here?

6. I looked everywhere for my pen.

7. The man stopped suddenly and quickly turned around.

8. Stacy read that poem too rapidly.

9. Janice plays the guitar well.

10. The child was sleeping soundly.

11. The car was running noisily.

12. We returned early.

13. Those trees were severely damaged in the fire.

14. Jack ran quickly, but steadily, in the race.

B. Write two adverbs that could be used to modify each verb.

1. read _____ _____

2. think _____ _____

3. walk _____ _____

4. eat _____ _____

5. sing _____ _____

6. speak _____ _____

7. dive _____ _____

8. study _____ _____

9. write _____ _____

10. look _____ _____

58 Comparing with Adverbs

LESSON

> - An **adverb** has three degrees of comparison: **positive**, **comparative**, and **superlative.**
> - The simple form of the adverb is called the **positive** degree.
>   EXAMPLE: Kathy ran **fast** in the race.
> - When two actions are being compared, the **comparative** degree is used.
>   EXAMPLE: Amy ran **faster** than Kathy.
> - When three or more actions are being compared, the **superlative** degree is used.
>   EXAMPLE: Maureen ran the **fastest** of all.
> - Use -er to form the comparative degree and use -est to form the superlative degree of one-syllable adverbs.
> - Use more or most with longer adverbs and with adverbs that end in -ly.
>   EXAMPLES: Louisa ran **more energetically** than Bob.
>   Ms. Baker ran the **most energetically** of all the runners.

A. Underline the adverb that best completes each sentence.

1. Mark arrived (sooner, soonest) than Greg.

2. Tony arrived the (sooner, soonest) of all.

3. They had to work very (hard, harder, hardest).

4. Tony painted (more, most) carefully than Mark.

5. Mark worked (faster, fastest) than Greg, so Mark painted the walls.

6. Lauren worked the (more, most) carefully of all.

B. Complete each sentence with the proper form of the adverb in parentheses.

1. (fast)   Jason wanted to run the _____ at our school.

2. (fast)   Juan could run _____ than Jason.

3. (seriously)   Jason trained _____ than he had before.

4. (frequently)   Jason is on the track _____ of all the runners.

5. (quickly)   Jason ran the sprint _____ than he did yesterday.

6. (promptly)   Jason arrives for practice _____ of anyone on the team.

7. (promptly)   He even arrives _____ than the coach!

8. (eagerly)   Juan does warm-up exercises _____ of all the runners.

9. (carefully)   Who concentrates _____ on his timing, Juan or Jason?

10. (hard)   The coach congratulates Jason on being the player who works the

_____.

Using Adjectives and Adverbs

■ **Underline the correct word.**

1. Always drive very (careful, carefully).

2. The lake seems (calm, calmly) today.

3. The storm raged (furious, furiously).

4. The dog waited (patient, patiently) for its owner.

5. Nicole's letters are always (cheerful, cheerfully) written.

6. Although our team played (good, well), we lost the game.

7. Always answer your mail (prompt, promptly).

8. James speaks (respectful, respectfully) to everyone.

9. Tara is (happy, happily) with her new work.

10. Write this address (legible, legibly).

11. The time passed (slow, slowly).

12. The robin chirped (happy, happily) from its nest.

13. We were (sure, surely) glad to hear from him.

14. Rebecca tries to do her work (good, well).

15. I think Brenda will (easy, easily) win that contest.

16. We had to talk (loud, loudly) to be heard.

17. Yesterday the sun shone (bright, brightly) all day.

18. He says he sleeps (good, well) every night.

19. The elevator went up (quick, quickly) to the top floor.

20. The storm began very (sudden, suddenly).

21. You did react very (cautious, cautiously).

22. Every student should do this work (accurate, accurately).

23. Eric rode his bike (furious, furiously) to get home on time.

24. The paint on the house is (new, newly).

25. The mist fell (steady, steadily) all evening.

26. The river looked (beautiful, beautifully) in the moonlight.

27. The salesperson always answers questions (courteous, courteously).

28. He always does (good, well) when selling that product.

29. Ryan can swim (good, well).

30. I was (real, really) excited about going to San Francisco.

31. I think he talks (foolish, foolishly).

32. It seems (foolish, foolishly) to me.

33. That bell rang too (loud, loudly) for this small room.

34. Our grass seems to grow very (rapid, rapidly).

Prepositions

LESSON 60

- A **preposition** is a word that shows the relationship of a noun or a pronoun to another word in the sentence.

  EXAMPLES: Put the package **on** the table. Place the package **in** the desk.
- These are some commonly used prepositions:

about	against	at	between	from	of	through	under
above	among	behind	by	in	on	to	upon
across	around	beside	for	into	over	toward	with

■ **Draw a line under each preposition or prepositions in the sentences below.**

1. The grin on Juan's face was bright and warm.

2. He greeted his cousin from Brazil with a smile and a handshake.

3. They walked through the airport and toward the baggage area.

4. Juan found his bags between two boxes.

5. The two cousins had not seen each other for five years.

6. They could spend hours talking about everything.

7. Juan and Luis got into Juan's truck.

8. Juan drove Luis to Juan's family's ranch.

9. It was a long ride across many hills and fields.

10. Luis rested his head against the seat.

11. Soon they drove over a hill and into a valley.

12. The ranch was located across the Harrison River.

13. The house stood among a group of oak trees.

14. Juan parked the truck beside the driveway.

15. They walked across the driveway and toward the house.

16. Juan's mother, Anita, stood behind the screen door.

17. Juan's family gathered around Luis.

18. Everyone sat on the porch and drank lemonade.

19. "Tell us about our relatives in Brazil," Rosa asked.

20. "You have over twenty cousins in my area," said Luis.

21. They go to school, just like you do.

22. Then everyone went into the house and ate dinner.

23. Juan's family passed the food across the table.

24. "Many of these dishes come from old family recipes," he said.

25. "It is wonderful to be among so many relatives," Luis said.

26. After dinner, everyone went to the living room.

27. Luis showed them photographs of his home in Brazil.

61 Prepositional Phrases

LESSON

- A **phrase** is a group of closely related words used as a single part of speech but not containing a subject and predicate.
    EXAMPLE: The writer **of this novel** is signing autographs.
- A **prepositional phrase** is a group of words that begins with a preposition and ends with a noun or pronoun.
    EXAMPLE: He took the train **to New York.**
- The noun or pronoun in the prepositional phrase is called the **object of the preposition.**
    EXAMPLE: He took the train to **New York.**

- **Put parentheses around each prepositional phrase. Then underline each preposition, and circle the object of the preposition.**

1. The airplane was flying (above the (clouds)).

2. We are moving to North Carolina.

3. Sandra lives on the second block.

4. An old water tower once stood on that hill.

5. The car slid on the wet pavement.

6. Sealing wax was invented in the seventeenth century.

7. Motto rings were first used by the Romans.

8. Tungsten, a metal, was discovered in 1781.

9. Roses originally came from Asia.

10. The ball rolled into the street.

11. Do you always keep the puppies in a pen?

12. The children climbed over the fence.

13. She lives in Denver, Colorado.

14. Columbus made three trips to North America.

15. They spread the lunch under the shade of the giant elm tree.

16. The treasure was found by a scuba diver.

17. A squad of soldiers marched behind the tank.

18. Shall I row across the stream?

19. Large airplanes fly across the nation.

20. Walter looked into the sack.

21. The cat ran up the pole.

22. We visited the Alexander Graham Bell Museum in Nova Scotia.

23. Many tourists come to our region.

24. We spent last summer in the Adirondack Mountains.

25. Do not stand behind a parked car.

Unit 3, Grammar and Usage

62 LESSON

Prepositional Phrases as Adjectives and Adverbs

> ■ A prepositional phrase can be used to describe a noun or a pronoun. Then the prepositional phrase is being used as an **adjective** to tell which one, what kind, or how many.
>   EXAMPLE: The bird **in the tree** whistled.
>   The prepositional phrase in the tree tells **which** bird.
> ■ A prepositional phrase can be used to describe a verb. Then the prepositional phrase is being used as an **adverb** to tell how, where, or when.
>   EXAMPLE: Charlie ate breakfast **before leaving for school.**
>   The prepositional phrase **before leaving for school** tells **when** Charlie ate breakfast.

■ **Underline each prepositional phrase, and classify it as adjective or adverb.**

1. They went to the ranch. *(adv.)*

2. The first savings bank was established in France.

3. Fall Creek Falls in Tennessee is my home.

4. Return all books to the public library.

5. Mark lives in an old house.

6. Tanya bought a sweater with red trim.

7. The birds in the zoo are magnificent.

8. Jade is found in Burma.

9. I spent the remainder of my money.

10. The magician waved a wand over the hat, and a rabbit appeared.

11. The diameter of a Sequoia tree trunk can reach ten feet.

12. The capital of New York is Albany.

13. The narrowest streets are near the docks.

14. Our family went to the movie.

15. Roald Amundsen discovered the South Pole in 1911.

16. The floor in this room is painted black.

17. The dead leaves are blowing across the yard.

18. A forest of petrified wood has been found.

19. The mole's tunnel runs across the lawn.

63
LESSON

Conjunctions

> - A **conjunction** is a word used to join words or groups of words.
>   EXAMPLE: Jenna **and** her sister are in Arizona.
> - These are some commonly used conjunctions:
>
> | | | | | | | |
> |---|---|---|---|---|---|---|
> | although | because | however | or | that | when | while |
> | and | but | if | since | though | whereas | yet |
> | as | for | nor | than | unless | whether | |
>
> - Some conjunctions are used in pairs. These include either . . .or, neither . . . nor, and not only . . . but also.

- **Underline each conjunction.**

1. He and I are friends.

2. David likes tennis, whereas Jim prefers running.

3. We had to wait since it was raining.

4. We left early, but we missed the train.

5. The show was not only long but also boring.

6. Neither the chairs nor the tables had been dusted.

7. Hail and sleet fell during the storm.

8. Neither Carmen nor Kara was able to attend the meeting.

9. I have neither time nor energy to waste.

10. Bowling and tennis are my favorite sports.

11. Either Dan or Don will bring a portable radio.

12. The people in the car and the people in the van exchanged greetings.

13. Neither cookies nor cake is on your diet.

14. Although I like to take photographs, I am not a good photographer.

15. Did you see Charles when he visited here?

16. We are packing our bags since our vacation trip begins tomorrow.

17. She cannot concentrate while you are making so much noise.

18. Unless you hurry, you will miss the party.

19. We enjoyed the visit although we were very tired.

20. Both mammals and birds are warm-blooded.

21. She is one performer who can both sing and dance.

22. Unless you have some objections, I will submit this report.

23. Neither dogs nor cats are allowed in this park.

24. April watered the plants while Luis mowed the lawn.

25. I will see you when you are feeling better.

26. Either Ms. Andretti or Ms. Garcia will teach that course.

27. We got here late because we lost our directions.

64

LESSON

Double Negatives

> ■ The **adverbs** <u>not</u>, <u>never</u>, <u>hardly</u>, scarcely, <u>seldom</u>, <u>none</u>, and <u>nothing</u> should not be used with a negative verb. One clause cannot properly contain two negatives.
>
> EXAMPLES: There wasn't anything left in the refrigerator. (Correct)
> There wasn't nothing left in the refrigerator. (Incorrect)

■ **Underline the correct word.**

1. We couldn't see (anything, nothing) through the fog.

2. The suspect wouldn't admit (anything, nothing).

3. I don't know (any, none) of the people on this bus.

4. Rosa couldn't do (anything, nothing) about changing the time of our program.

5. We didn't have (any, no) printed programs.

6. I don't want (any, no) cereal for breakfast this morning.

7. You must not speak to (anyone, no one) about our surprise party plans.

8. There isn't (any, no) ink in this pen.

9. Didn't you make (any, no) copies for the other people?

10. I haven't had (any, no) time to repair the lawn mower.

11. She hasn't said (anything, nothing) about her accident.

12. Hardly (anything, nothing) pleases him.

13. There aren't (any, no) pears in this supermarket.

14. There isn't (any, no) newspaper in that little town.

15. There wasn't (anybody, nobody) in the house.

16. Please don't ask him (any, no) questions.

17. I haven't solved (any, none) of my problems.

18. I haven't done (anything, nothing) to offend Greg.

19. We don't have (any, no) water pressure.

20. Our team wasn't (any, no) match for the opposing team.

21. I couldn't hear (anything, nothing) because of the airplane's noise.

22. The salesperson didn't have (any, no) samples on display.

23. I haven't (any, no) money with me.

24. Hasn't he cooked (any, none) of the pasta?

25. We haven't (any, no) more packages to wrap.

26. Wasn't there (anyone, no one) at home?

27. My dog has never harmed (anybody, nobody).

28. They seldom have (anyone, no one) absent from their meetings.

29. There weren't (any, no) clouds in the sky.

Review

A. Write the part of speech above each underlined word. Use the abbreviations given in the box.

1. A heavy dust storm rolled across the prairie.

2. This is a nice surprise!

3. The dark clouds slowly gathered in the north.

4. Marlee and I are showing slides of the photographs that we took on our trip.

5. Is the capital of your state built on a river?

6. These shrubs are beautiful.

7. Someone opened the door very cautiously and tiptoed inside.

8. Please handle this extremely fragile china very carefully.

9. The weary people waited for the long parade to start.

10. Large herds of longhorn cattle grazed on these vast plains.

11. We are going to the new mall today, but Sara can't go with us.

12. Floyd, you are eating that food too rapidly.

n.	noun
pron.	pronoun
v.	verb
adj.	adjective
adv.	adverb
prep.	preposition
conj.	conjunction

B. Write the plural form or the possessive form of the noun in parentheses.

1. (bench)   The park _____ need to be painted.

2. (fly)   The _____ landed on our picnic lunch.

3. (hero)   All of the _____ medals were awarded at the ceremony.

4. (pony)   Her _____ saddle has been cleaned and oiled.

5. (watch)   My _____ hands stopped moving.

C. Underline the appositive or appositive phrase, and circle the noun it identifies.

1. We plan to visit Ottawa, the capital of Canada, on our vacation.

2. My older sister Kira is an engineer.

3. We ate a hearty breakfast, pancakes and ham, before going to work.

D. Circle the correct verb.

1. A former resident (gave, given) this fountain to the city.

2. Was it the telephone or the doorbell that (rang, rung)?

3. Our guest speaker has (come, came) a little early.

4. Caroline has (know, known) Paul for ten years.

5. We asked Jan to (drive, driven) us to the movies.

6. Matt, haven't you (ate, eaten) the last piece of pineapple cake?

7. The frightened deer (ran, run) into the forest.

8. The Arnolds (gone, went) to Florida last January.

9. Andy (doesn't, don't) like to be late to work.

10. Chloe (took, taken) her brother to the zoo.

11. Susan (did, done) all of her chores before we went to the movie.

12. Jessica and I (is, are) ready to go, too.

13. Many of the trout (was, were) returned to the stream after the contest.

14. I have (began, begun) the study of Spanish.

15. A dead silence had (fell, fallen) upon the listeners.

16. Larry (wasn't, weren't) at work this morning.

E. Underline the verbal in each sentence, and write <u>infinitive</u>, <u>participle</u>, or <u>gerund</u> on the line.

_____ 1. The reason they went to the lake was to fish.

_____ 2. Skating has become a popular sport.

_____ 3. The flashing lights warned people of danger.

_____ 4. Juan's goal is to finish law school.

_____ 5. The improved detergent cleaned better than the old formula.

F. Underline the pronoun in parentheses that agrees with the antecedent. Circle the antecedent.

1. Curtis and Erika tutored Mark because (he, they) had missed the review.

2. The office workers had to leave (their, its) building when a fire started.

3. Bob and Andre brought the posters to (them, their) campaign office.

4. My sister collected baskets on (her, their) trip to Mexico.

5. The volunteers accepted donations and gave (it, them) to the charity.

Using What You've Learned

A. Read the following paragraphs.

Tibet, which is a remote land in south-central Asia, is often called the Roof of the World or Land of the Snows. Its mountains and plateaus are the highest in the world. The capital of Tibet, Lhasa, is 12,000 feet high.

Tibetans, who are sometimes called the hermit people, follow a simple way of life. They are a short and sturdy people and do heavy physical work. Some are nomads, herders who roam about in the northern uplands of the country. Once a year, the nomads come to the low regions to sell their products and to buy things that they need. They live in tents made of yak hair. A yak is about the size of a small ox and has long hair. Yaks are good companions to the nomads because they can live and work in the high altitudes.

B. Write two appositives from the paragraph above.

_____   _____

C. Write four relative pronouns and their antecedents.

1. _____ _____   3. _____ _____

2. _____ _____   4. _____ _____

D. Write three prepositional phrases.

1. _____

2. _____

3. _____

E. Write one superlative adjective.

_____

F. Write one indefinite pronoun.

_____

G. Write two intransitive verbs.

_____   _____

H. Write two infinitives.

_____   _____

I. Write two conjunctions.

_____   _____

J. Read the following paragraphs.

If you were to guess which people were the first to learn to write, would you guess the Egyptians? Experts believe thousands of years ago, around 3100 B.C., Egyptians first began writing. Much of their writing was done to record historical events. Later, writings were used on pyramids to ensure peace for the kings buried in them. The writings were in hieroglyphics, a system of writing based on pictures.

Egyptian pyramids are notable for a number of reasons. The oldest pyramid is called Saqqarah. It was built with hundreds of steps running up to the top and was the first building in the country made entirely of stone. It clearly shows how advanced the ancient Egyptian culture was, both artistically and mechanically.

Another incredible monument is the Great Sphinx—a half-lion, half-man stone structure built for King Khafre. Historians have been able to learn much about the ancient Egyptian people by studying these buildings and the materials in them. Fortunately, the climate in Egypt was dry, so the writings and artifacts were well-preserved.

K. Write a subjunctive verb from the paragraph above.

_____

L. Write two adverbs.

_____   _____

M. Write two passive verbs.

_____   _____

N. Write an appositive.

_____

O. Write two abstract nouns.

_____   _____

P. Write two concrete nouns.

_____   _____

Q. Write two conjunctions.

_____   _____

R. Write two prepositional phrases.

_____

_____

Using Capital Letters

- **Capitalize** the first word of a sentence and of each line of poetry.
  - EXAMPLES: Jim recited a poem. The first two lines follow.
    All the animals looked up in wonder
    When they heard the roaring thunder.
- Capitalize the first word of a direct quotation.
  - EXAMPLE: Beth said, "Let's try to memorize a poem, too."
- Capitalize the first, last, and all important words in the titles of books, poems, stories, and songs.
  - EXAMPLES: *The Jungle Book,* "Snow Time"

A. Circle each letter that should be capitalized. Write the capital letter above it.

1. Anthony said, "what time does the movie start?"

2. francis Scott Key wrote "the star spangled banner."

3. edgar Allan Poe, the author of "the raven," was born in Boston.

4. paul asked, "when do you plan to visit your friend?"

5. who wrote the poems "snowbound" and "the barefoot boy"?

6. what famous American said, "give me liberty, or give me death"?

- Capitalize all **proper nouns.**
  - EXAMPLES: James T. White, Mother, Fifth Avenue, Italy, Missouri Smokey Mountains, Thanksgiving, November, Statue of Liberty, *Mayflower,* British Columbia
- Capitalize all **proper adjectives.** A proper adjective is an adjective that is made from a proper noun.
  - EXAMPLES: the Italian language, Chinese food, French tourists

B. Circle each letter that should be capitalized. Write the capital letter above it.

1. Lauren, does your friend live in miami, florida, or atlanta, georgia?

2. The potomac river forms the boundary between virginia and maryland.

3. The *pinta,* the *niña,* and the *santa maría* were the ships columbus sailed.

4. The spanish explorers discovered the mississippi river before the english settlers

   landed at jamestown.

5. The founder of the american red cross was clara barton.

6. Glaciers are found in the rocky mountains, the andes mountains, and the alps.

> ■ Capitalize a person's title when it comes before a name.
>   EXAMPLES: Mayor Flynn, Doctor Suarez, Governor Kuhn
> ■ Capitalize abbreviations of titles.
>   EXAMPLES: Ms. C. Cooke, Dr. Pearsoll, Gov. Milne, Judge Brenner

C. Circle each letter that should be capitalized. Write the capital letter above it.

1. How long have you been seeing dr. thompson?

2. Our class invited mayor thomas to speak at graduation.

3. dr. crawford w. long of Georgia is believed to be the first physician to

   use ether during surgery.

4. What time do you expect mr. and mrs. randall to arrive?

5. Most people believe senator dixon will win reelection.

6. It will be a close election unless gov. alden gives his support.

7. When is ms. howell scheduled to begin teaching?

> ■ Capitalize abbreviations of days and months, parts of addresses, and
>   titles of members of the armed forces. Also capitalize all letters in the
>   abbreviations of states.
>   EXAMPLES: Tues.; Nov.; 201 S. Main St.; Maj. Donna C. Plunkett;
>   Boston, MA

D. Circle each letter that should be capitalized. Write the capital letter above it.

1. niles school art fair

   sat., feb. 8th, 9 A.M.

   110 n. elm dr.

2. shoreville water festival

   june 23–24

   mirror lake

   shoreville, mn 55108

3. october fest

   october 28 and 29

   9 A.M.–5 P.M.

   63 maple st.

4. barbara dumont

   150 telson rd.

   markham, ontario L3R 1E5

5. captain c. j. neil

   c/o *ocean star*

   p.o. box 4455

   portsmouth, nh 03801

6. dr. charles b. stevens

   elmwood memorial hospital

   1411 first street

   tucson, az 85062

66 LESSON
Using End Punctuation

■ Use a **period** at the end of a declarative sentence.
  EXAMPLE: Sunlight is essential for the growth of plants.
■ Use a **question mark** at the end of an interrogative sentence.
  EXAMPLE: How much sunlight does a plant need?

A. Use a period or question mark to end each sentence below.

1. Doesn't Sandra's family now live in Missouri____

2. "Snow Time" is a well-known poem____

3. Isn't someone knocking at the door, Beth____

4. Didn't Janice ask us to meet her at 2:30 this afternoon____

5. In Yellowstone Park, we saw Morning Glory Pool, Handkerchief Pool, and Old Faithful____

6. The greatest library in ancient times was in Alexandria, Egypt____

7. Aren't the employees' checks deposited in a different bank____

8. Will Ms. Wilson start interviewing applicants at 10:00 A.M.____

9. My uncle has moved to Calgary, Alberta____

10. Corn, oats, and soybeans are grown in Iowa____

11. Isn't Alex the chairperson of our committee____

12. I've mowed the lawn, pulled the weeds, and raked the leaves____

13. Did the American Revolution begin on April 19, 1775____

14. Is El Salvador in Central America____

B. Add the correct end punctuation where needed in the paragraphs below.

Did you know that experts say dogs have been around for thousands of years____ In fact, they were the first animals to be made domestic____ The ancestors of dogs were hunters____ Wolves are related to domestic dogs____ Like wolves, dogs are social animals and prefer to travel in groups____ This is called pack behavior____

There have been many famous dogs throughout history____ Can you name any of them____ In the eleventh century, one dog, Saur, was named king of Norway____ The actual king was angry because his people had removed him from the throne, so he decided to make them subjects of the dog____ The first dog in space was a Russian dog named Laika____ Laika was aboard for the 1957 journey of *Sputnik*____ Most people have heard of Rin Tin Tin and Lassie____ These dogs became famous in movies and television____

There are several hundred breeds of dogs throughout the world____ The smallest is the Chihuahua____ A Chihuahua weighs less than two pounds____ Can you think of the largest____ A Saint Bernard or a Mastiff can weigh over 150 pounds____

67
LESSON

Using Commas

- Use a **comma** between words or groups of words that are in a series.
  EXAMPLE: Pears, peaches, plums, and figs grow in the southern states.
- Use a comma before a conjunction in a compound sentence.
  EXAMPLE: The farmers planted many crops, and they will work long hours to harvest them.
- Use a comma after a subordinate clause when it begins a sentence.
  EXAMPLE: After we ate dinner, we went to a movie.

A. Add commas where needed in the sentences below.

1. Frank Mary and Patricia are planning a surprise party for their parents.

2. It is their parents' fiftieth wedding anniversary and the children want it to be special.

3. They have invited the people their father used to work with their mother's garden club members and long-time friends of the family.

4. Even though the children are grown and living in their own homes it will be hard to make it a surprise.

5. Mr. and Mrs. Slaughter are active friendly and involved in many things.

6. For the surprise to work everyone will have to be sure not to say anything about their plans for that day.

7. This will be especially hard for the Knudsens but they will do their best.

8. Since every Sunday the families have dinner together the Knudsens will have to become very good actors the week of the party.

- Use a comma to set off a quotation from the rest of a sentence.
  EXAMPLES: "I want to go with you," said Paul.
  Paul said, "I want to go with you."

B. Add commas before or after the quotations below.

1. "We're sorry that we have to cancel our plans" said Earl.

2. Carmen said "But we've done this every week for ten years!"

3. Jeanette said "We have to leave town."

4. Ivan asked "Can't you put it off just one day?"

5. "No I'm afraid we can't" said Earl.

6. "Then we'll just start over the following week" said Carmen cheerfully.

7. Jeanette said "I bet no one else has done this."

8. "I sure hate to spoil our record" said Earl.

9. "Don't worry about it" said Ivan.

10. "Yes everything will work out" said Jeanette.

> ■ Use a comma to set off the name of a person who is being addressed.
>   EXAMPLE: Philip, would you like to leave now?
> ■ Use a comma to set off words like yes, no, well, oh, first, next, and finally
>   at the beginning of a sentence.
>   EXAMPLE: Well, we better get going.
> ■ Use a comma to set off an appositive.
>   EXAMPLE: Alan, Philip's brother, is a doctor in Saint Louis.

C. Add commas where needed in the sentences below.

1. Dr. Perillo a nutritionist is an expert on proper eating.

2. "Students it's important to eat a well-balanced diet," she said.

3. "Yes but how do we know what the right foods are?" asked one student.

4. "First you need to look carefully at your eating habits," said Dr. Perillo.

5. "Yes you will keep a journal of the foods you eat," she said.

6. "Dr. Perillo what do you mean by the right servings?" asked Emilio.

7. "Okay good question," she said.

8. "A serving Emilio is a certain amount of a food," said Dr. Perillo.

9. "Dave a cross-country runner will need more calories than a less
   active student," explained Dr. Perillo.

10. "Class remember to eat foods from the five basic food groups," she said.

D. Add commas where needed in the paragraphs below.

Our neighbor Patrick has fruit trees on his property. "Patrick what
kinds of fruit do you grow?" I asked. "Well I grow peaches apricots
pears and plums" he replied. "Wow! That's quite a variety" I said.
Patrick's son Jonathan helps his dad care for the trees. "Oh it's constant
work and care" Jonathan said "but the delicious results are worth the
effort." After harvesting the fruit Jonathan's mother Allison cans the fruit
for use throughout the year. She makes preserves and she gives them
as gifts for special occasions. Allison sells some of her preserves to
Chris Simon the owner of a local shop. People come from all over the
county to buy Allison's preserves.

Jonathan's aunt Christina grows corn tomatoes beans and squash in
her garden. Each year she selects her best vegetables and enters them
in the fair. She has won blue ribbons medals and certificates for her
vegetables. "Oh I just like being outside. That's why I enjoy gardening"
Christina said. Christina's specialty squash-and-tomato bread is one of the
most delicious breads I have ever tasted.

Using Quotation Marks and Apostrophes

LESSON 68

> - Use **quotation marks** to show the exact words of a speaker. Use a comma or another punctuation mark to separate the quotation from the rest of the sentence.
>   EXAMPLES: "Do you have a book on helicopters?" asked Tom.
>   James said, "It's right here."
> - A quotation may be placed at the beginning or at the end of a sentence. It may also be divided within the sentence.
>   EXAMPLES: Deborah said, "There are sixty active members."
>   "Morton," asked Juanita, "have you read this magazine article?"

A. Add quotation marks and other punctuation where needed in the sentences below.

1. Dan, did you ever play football asked Tim.

2. Morris asked Why didn't you come in for an interview?

3. I have never said Laurie heard a story about a ghost.

4. Selina said Yuri thank you for the present.

5. When do we start on our trip to the mountains asked Stan.

6. Our guest said You don't know how happy I am to be in your house.

7. My sister said Kelly bought those beautiful baskets in Mexico.

8. I'm going to plant the spinach said Doris as soon as I get home.

> - Use an **apostrophe** in a contraction to show where a letter or letters have been taken out.
>   EXAMPLES: Amelia **didn't** answer the phone. **I've** found my wallet.
> - Use an apostrophe to form a possessive noun. Add -'s to most singular nouns. Add -' to most plural nouns. Add -'s to a few nouns that have irregular plurals.
>   EXAMPLES: A **child's** toy was in our yard. The **girls'** toys were in our yard. The **children's** toys were in our yard.

B. After each sentence below, write the word in which an apostrophe has been left out. Add the apostrophe where needed.

1. Many players uniforms are red. _____

2. That dog played with the babys shoe. _____

3. Julio isnt coming with us to the library. _____

4. Its very warm for a fall day. _____

5. The captains ship was one of the newest. _____

6. Marcia doesnt sing as well as my sister does. _____

7. Mens coats are sold in the new store. _____

69 LESSON

Using Other Punctuation

> ■ Use a **hyphen** between the parts of some compound words.
> EXAMPLE: poverty-stricken   sixty-three   two-thirds
> part-time   able-bodied   brother-in-law
> hard-boiled   short-term   red-hot
> ■ Use a hyphen to separate the syllables of a word that is carried over from one line to the next.
> EXAMPLE: So many things were going on at once that no one could possibly guess how the play would end.

A. Add hyphens where needed in the sentences below.

1. The play was going to be in an old fashioned theater.

2. The theater was so small that there were seats for only ninety two people.

3. The vice president was played by Alan Lowe.

> ■ Use a **colon** after the greeting in a business letter.
> EXAMPLES: Dear Mr. Johnson: Dear Sirs:
> ■ Use a colon between the hour and the minute when writing the time.
> EXAMPLES: 1:30   6:15   11:47
> ■ Use a colon to introduce a list.
> EXAMPLE: Our grocery list included the following items: chicken, milk, eggs, and broccoli.

B. Add colons where needed in the sentences below.

1. At 2 1 0 this afternoon, the meeting will start.

2. Please bring the following materials with you pencils, paper, erasers, and a notebook.

3. The meeting should be over by 4 3 0.

4. Those of you on the special committee should bring the following items cups, paper plates, forks, spoons, and napkins.

> ■ Use a **semicolon** between the clauses of a compound sentence that are closely related but not connected by a conjunction. Do not capitalize the word after a semicolon.
> EXAMPLE: Hummingbirds and barn swallows migrate; most sparrows live in one place all year.

C. In the sentences below, add semicolons where needed.

1. Colleen is a clever teacher she is also an inspiring one.

2. Her lectures are interesting they are full of information.

3. She has a college degree in history world history is her specialty.

4. She begins her classes by answering questions she ends them by asking questions.

Review

A. Circle each letter that should be capitalized. Then add the correct end punctuation.

1. mr. j. c. moran owns a car dealership in chicago, illinois____

2. jesse decided to apply for a job on tuesday____

3. wow, mr. moran actually offered him a job____

4. jesse will start work in june____

5. jesse is the newest employee of moran's cars and vans____

6. didn't he get auto experience when he lived in minnesota____

7. he also got training at dunwoody technical institute____

8. jesse took some computer courses there taught by mr. ted woods and ms. jane hart____

9. jesse had only temporary jobs at highland cafe and mayfield electronics for the last two years____

10. since jesse wants to be prepared for his new job, he checked out *automobile technology and the automobile industry* from the windham library____

B. Add commas where needed in the sentences below.

1. After Jesse got the new job his family friends and neighbors gave him a party.

2. Everyone brought food drinks and even some gifts.

3. Bob Jesse's roommate and Carmen Jesse's sister bought him a briefcase.

4. His mother and father bought him a new shirt jacket and tie for his first day on the job.

5. His father congratulated him by saying "Jesse we are happy for you and we wish you the best in your new job."

6. Jesse replied "Well I'm also very excited about it and I want to thank all of you for the party and the gifts."

C. Add commas and quotation marks where needed in the sentences below.

1. How did you get so lucky Jesse? asked Mike.

2. It wasn't luck answered Jesse because I studied before I applied for this job.

3. I didn't know you could study to apply for a job said Mike laughing.

4. Mike I read an employment guide before I applied said Jesse.

5. I have never heard of an employment guide! exclaimed Mike.

6. It's a great book said Jesse.

7. Jesse I'd like to apply for a job at Moran's said Mike.

8. Jesse replied Why don't you read my guide to prepare for the interview?

D. Insert apostrophes, colons, and hyphens where needed in the sentences below.

1. Joe King, Jesses best friend, is the one who gave Jesse the employment guide to use for his interview at Morans.

2. Jesse didnt know important interview skills.

3. The guide offered twenty five helpful hints.

4. The guide suggested the following dress neatly, be on time, be polite, and be enthusiastic.

5. Jesse also used the guides suggestions for preparing a resume listing his work experience.

6. Jesses list contained these items his employers names and addresses, dates of employment, and job descriptions.

7. The guide said Jesse should be a well informed applicant, so he researched salespersons duties and made a list of questions to ask.

8. Jesses guide recommended getting to the interview early to have time to fill out the employers application forms.

9. Jesse arrived at Mr. Morans office at 345 for his 400 interview.

10. The interview lasted forty five minutes, and Jesse was relaxed and self confident when he left.

11. Mr. Morans phone call the next day at 130 let Jesse know he had gotten the job.

12. Jesse needed to do the following pick up a salespersons manual, fill out employment forms, and enroll in the companys insurance program.

E. Punctuate the letter below. Circle each letter that should be capitalized.

73 e. river st.

chicago, il 65067

may 30, 2005

Dear mr. moran:

    I just wanted to thank you for offering me the salespersons position with your company ____ you mentioned in our interview that my duties would be the following selling cars and vans checking customers credit references and assisting customers with their paperwork ____ ive studied the automobile sales guide that you gave me and i feel that im prepared to do a terrific job for morans ____ thank you again im looking forward to starting next monday ____

                sincerely,

                jesse sanchez

Using What You've Learned

A. Add punctuation where needed in the paragraphs below. Circle each letter that should be capitalized. Be sure to underline book titles.

have you ever heard the story called "the dog and his bone"___ there once was a dog that had a new bone___ this is a great bone said the dog to himself___ the dog decided to take a walk and carried the bone proudly in its mouth___ he went down a dirt road and over a bridge___ as he was crossing the bridge he looked down into the river___ wow said the dog look at that big bone in the water___ the dog thought to himself id rather have that bone than the one i have right now___ can you guess what happened next___ well the dog opened his mouth and dropped the bone–a foolish thing to do–into the river___ when the splash of the bone hitting the water stopped the dog looked for the bigger bone___ however he didnt see it anymore___ what he did see was his old bone sinking to the bottom of the river___

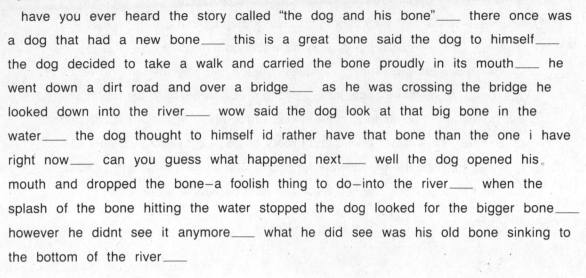

there is an incredible man scott targot who lives in my town___ his nickname is the ironman___ people call him ironman targot because he has won several triathlons___ do you know what a triathlon is___ some people consider it the ultimate sports contest___ athletes have to swim for 2.4 miles ride a bike for 112 miles and run for 26.2 miles___ just one of those alone is a lot of work___ scott will train from february to august in preparation for a triathlon in hawaii___ scott says i wouldnt want to be doing anything else with my time___ each day during training he gets up at 7 0 0 loosens up for a half hour then runs from 7 3 0 to 8 3 0___ after he cools down a little he takes a 20 mile bike ride___ at the end of the ride he swims for an hour and a half___ yes i get tired he says but i usually feel refreshed after swimming___ last he lifts light weights and takes a break to do some reading___

a triathlon is supposed to be completed in less than seventeen hours___ the record is less than half that time___ thats my goal says scott___ hes still trying to break 14 hours and ten minutes___ scotts usually one of the top finishers___

B. Rewrite the story below. Be sure to use capital letters and punctuation marks where they are needed.

sir walter scott one of the worlds greatest storytellers was born in edinburgh, scotland, on august 15, 1771____ walter had an illness just before he was two years old that left him lame for the rest of his life____ his par ents were worried so they sent him to his grandparents farm in sandy knowe____ they thought the country air would do him good____

walters parents were right____ he was quite healthy by the time he was six years old____ he was happy, too____ walter loved listening to his grandfather tell stories about scotland____ the stories stirred his imagination____ he began to read fairy tales travel books and history books____ it was these ear ly stories that laid the groundwork for Scotts later interest in writing stories____ his most famous book *Ivanhoe* has been read by people around the world____

_____

_____

_____

_____

_____

_____

_____

_____

_____

_____

_____

_____

_____

_____

_____

_____

Check What You've Learned

A. Write <u>S</u> before each pair of synonyms, <u>A</u> before each pair of antonyms, and <u>H</u> before each pair of homonyms.

_____ **1.** mean, cruel   _____ **3.** terrible, wonderful

_____ **2.** bread, bred   _____ **4.** sore, soar

B. Write the homograph for the pair of meanings.

_____ **1.** to shake   **2.** a glass container

C. Write <u>P</u> before each word with a prefix, <u>S</u> before each word with a suffix, and <u>C</u> before each compound word.

_____ **1.** thoughtful   _____ **3.** unconventional

_____ **2.** handlebar   _____ **4.** undercover

D. Write the words that make up each contraction.

_____ _____ **1.** I'd   _____ _____ **2.** don't

E. Underline the word in parentheses that has the more negative connotation.

The concert was (unpleasant, horrible).

F. Circle the number of the idiom that means <u>undecided</u>.

1. up in the air   **2.** off the wall

G. Write <u>D</u> before the declarative sentence, <u>IM</u> before the imperative sentence, <u>E</u> before the exclamatory sentence, and <u>IN</u> before the interrogative sentence. Then underline the simple subject, and circle the simple predicate in each sentence.

_____ **1.** Hey, that isn't yours!   _____ **3.** I am watching the evening news.

_____ **2.** Read me the next question.   _____ **4.** Who wanted the tuna sandwich?

H. Write <u>CS</u> before the sentence that has a compound subject and <u>CP</u> before the sentence that has a compound predicate.

_____ **1.** Kiwis and mangoes are unusual fruits.

_____ **2.** The ocean waves pounded and sprayed the beach.

I. Write <u>CS</u> before the compound sentence. Write <u>RO</u> before the run-on sentence. Write <u>I</u> before the sentence that is in inverted order.

_____ **1.** Bart loves to swim, and he teaches children's swimming classes.

_____ **2.** On the board the next assignment she wrote.

_____ **3.** It was over in an instant, no one saw what had happened.

J. Put brackets around the subordinate clause, and underline the independent clause in this complex sentence. Then write <u>DO</u> above the direct object.

Dana gave her the box of chocolates that someone had sent.

K. Underline the common nouns, and circle the proper nouns in the sentence.

Before Edward could stop his car, Mr. Huang opened the door and jumped out.

L. Circle the appositive in the sentence. Underline the noun it identifies or explains.

Our local newspaper, *The Hunterstown Gazette,* is the oldest in the state.

M. Write past, present, or future to show the tense of each underlined verb.

1. _____ Yolanda went shopping yesterday.

2. _____ Do you know the answer?

3. _____ It will be dark before he gets here.

4. _____ Rain was predicted for the weekend.

N. Circle the correct verbs in each sentence.

1. It (begun, began) to rain before we (eat, ate).

2. (Learning, Teaching) someone how to rollerblade has (be, been) fun.

3. I (taken, took) my time and (chose, choose) wisely.

4. He (set, sat) his glasses on the table when he (lay, laid) down.

O. Circle the number of the sentence that is in the active voice.

1. James threw the basketball through the hoop.

2. Her brother was expected on the next train.

P. Write SP before the sentence that has a subject pronoun, OP before the sentence that has an object pronoun, PP before the sentence that has a possessive pronoun, and IP before the sentence that has an indefinite pronoun. Circle the pronoun in each sentence.

1. _____ We knew the movie had already begun.

2. _____ Sally told her to hang the clothes in the closet.

3. _____ Stephanie and Frank spent their vacation in Montreal.

4. _____ Someone must have seen where the dog went.

Q. Underline the pronoun. Circle its antecedent.

Annette served the wonderful dinner with her customary flair.

R. On the line before each sentence, write adjective or adverb to describe the underlined word.

1. _____ Jack is the calmest dog I have ever known.

2. _____ The group listened intently to the speech.

3. _____ The bicycle was an antique.

4. _____ He ran faster than anyone else.

5. _____ Her car had two flat tires.

6. _____ The children were exceptionally polite at the dinner.

S. Underline each prepositional phrase twice, and circle each preposition. Underline each conjunction once.

Hoan pretended to be asleep when his father came into his room to wake him for breakfast.

Check What You've Learned

T. Rewrite the letter. Add capital letters and punctuation where needed.

482 w. franklin st.
overhill mt 80897
aug 22 2005

dear ms muller___

i received the application you sent me but these enclosures were not included the aptitude test the self addressed envelope and the postcard___ would you please send them as soon as possible___ i want to complete everything just as you want it___

id like to confirm our appointment for wednesday september 14 at 315 P.M. i look forward to seeing you then and talking with you about the scholarship___

yours truly___

roy thompson

Check What You've Learned Correlation Chart

Below is a list of the sections on *Check What You've Learned* and the pages on which the skills in each section are taught. If you missed any questions, turn to the pages listed and practice the skills. Then correct the problems you missed on *Check What You've Learned*.

Section	Skill	Practice Page
	Unit 1 Vocabulary	
A	Synonyms and Antonyms	5
	Homonyms	6
B	Homographs	7
C	Prefixes	8
	Suffixes	9
	Compound Words	11
D	Contractions	10
E	Connotation/Denotation	12
F	Idioms	13
	Unit 2 Sentences	
G	Types of Sentences	19
	Simple Subjects and Predicates	22
H	Compound Subjects	24
	Compound Predicates	25
	Combining Sentences	26
I	Position of Subjects	23
	Compound and Complex Sentences	31–32
	Correcting Run-on Sentences	33
J	Direct Objects	27
	Independent and Subordinate Clauses	29
	Compound and Complex Sentences	31
	Unit 3 Grammar and Usage	
K	Common and Proper Nouns	39
L	Appositives	44
M	Verb Phrases	46
N	Using *Is/Are* and *Was/Were*	49
	Past Tenses of *See*, *Go*, and *Begin*	50
	Past Tenses of *Freeze*, *Choose*, *Speak*, and *Break*	51

Section	Skill	Practice Page
	Unit 3 Grammar and Usage	
N	*Come*, *Ring*, *Drink*, *Know*, and *Throw*	52
	Past Tenses of *Give*, *Take*, and *Write*	53
	Eat, *Fall*, *Draw*, *Drive*, and *Run*	54
	Forms of *Do*	55
	Using *May/Can* and *Teach/Learn*	62
	Using *Sit/Set* and *Lay/Lie*	63
O	Active and Passive Voice	58
P	Pronouns	64
	Demonstrative and Indefinite Pronouns	65
	Relative Pronouns	67
Q	Pronouns	64
	Antecedents	66
R	Adjectives	69
	Demonstrative Adjectives	70
	Comparing with Adjectives	71
	Adverbs	72
	Comparing with Adverbs	73
	Using Adjectives and Adverbs	74
S	Prepositions	75
	Prepositional Phrases	76
	Conjunctions	78
	Unit 4 Capitalization and Punctuation	
T	Using Capital Letters	84–85
	Using End Punctuation	86
	Using Commas	87–88
	Using Quotation Marks and Apostrophes	89
	Using Other Punctuation	90

Language Terms

abstract noun names an idea, quality, action, or feeling

active voice a sentence in which the subject acts

adjective modifies a noun

adverb modifies a verb, an adjective, or another adverb

antecedent the word to which a pronoun refers

antonym has the opposite meaning of another word

apostrophe a mark used to show where a letter or letters have been left out of a contraction

appositive a noun or phrase that identifies or explains the noun it follows

clause a group of words that contains a subject and a predicate

collective noun names a group of persons or things

common noun names any one of a class of objects

complete predicate the part of a sentence that includes all the words that state action or condition of the subject

complete subject the part of a sentence that includes all the words that tell who or what the sentence is about

complex sentence contains one independent clause and one or more subordinate clauses

compound predicate two or more simple predicates

compound sentence two or more independent clauses

compound subject two or more simple subjects

compound word a word made up of two or more words

concrete noun names things you can see and touch

conjunction a word used to join words or groups of words

connotation suggests something positive or negative

contraction a word formed by joining two other words

declarative sentence a sentence that makes a statement

demonstrative adjective points out a specific person or thing

demonstrative pronoun points out a specific person or thing

denotation the exact meaning of a word

descriptive adjective tells *what kind*, *which one*, or *how many*

direct object who or what receives the action of the verb

exclamatory sentence expresses strong emotion

gerund a verb form ending in *-ing* used as a noun

helping verb used to help the main verb of the sentence

homograph has the same spelling as another word, but a different meaning and sometimes a different pronunciation

homonym sounds like another word, but has a different meaning and is spelled differently

idiom an expression that has a meaning different from the usual meanings of the individual words within it

imperative mood expresses a command or a request

imperative sentence expresses a command or a request

indefinite pronoun does not refer to a specific person or thing

independent clause a clause that can stand alone as a sentence because it expresses a complete thought

indicative mood states a fact or asks a question

indirect object tells to whom or for whom an action is done

infinitive the base form of the verb, usually preceded by *to*

interrogative sentence a sentence that asks a question

intransitive verb does not need an object

inverted order the order of a sentence when all or part of the predicate comes before the subject

limiting adjective the articles *a*, *an*, and *the*

mood verb form that shows the manner of doing or being

natural order the order of a sentence when the subject comes before all or part of the predicate

noun a word that names a person, place, thing, or quality

object of the preposition noun or pronoun in the prepositional phrase

object pronoun used after an action verb or preposition

participle a present or past tense verb used as an adjective

passive voice a sentence in which the subject receives the action

possessive noun shows possession of the noun that follows

possessive pronoun used to show ownership

predicate tells what the subject does or what happens to the subject

prefix a syllable added to the beginning of a base word that changes the meaning of the word

preposition a word that shows the relationship of a noun or a pronoun to another word in the sentence

prepositional phrase a group of words that begins with a preposition and ends with a noun or pronoun

pronoun a word that takes the place of a noun

proper adjective adjective formed from a proper noun

proper noun a noun that names a particular person, place, or thing and is capitalized

relative pronoun a pronoun that can introduce a subordinate clause

run-on sentence two or more independent clauses that are run together without correct punctuation

sentence expresses a complete thought

simple predicate the verb in the complete predicate

simple sentence contains only one independent clause

simple subject the main word in the complete subject

subject tells who or what the sentence is about

subject pronoun a pronoun used in the subject of a sentence and after a linking verb

subjunctive mood can indicate a wish or a contrary-to-fact condition

subordinate clause has a subject and predicate but is not a sentence because it does not express a complete thought

suffix a syllable added to the end of a base word that changes the meaning of the word

synonym a word that has the same or nearly the same meaning as one or more other words

transitive verb has a direct object

verb a word that expresses action, being, or state of being

verb phrase a main verb and one or more helping verbs

verb tense tells the time of the action or being

voice relation of a subject to the action expressed by the verb

Personal Pronouns						
	Singular			**Plural**		
	Subject Pronouns	Possessive Pronouns	Object Pronouns	Subject Pronouns	Possessive Pronouns	Object Pronouns
First Person	I	my, mine	me	we	our, ours	us
Second Person	you	your, yours	you	you	your, yours	you
Third Person	he	his	him	they	their, theirs	them
	she	her, hers	her	they	their, theirs	them
	it	its	it	they	their, theirs	them
First person is the person speaking or writing. Second person is the person spoken to or written to. Third person is the person spoken about or written about.						

Irregular Verbs

Present Tense	Past Tense	Past Participle	Present Tense	Past Tense	Past Participle
be	was, were	been	lay	laid	laid
begin	began	begun	lead	led	led
bite	bit	bitten	leave	left	left
blow	blew	blown	let	let	let
break	broke	broken	lie	lay	lain
bring	brought	brought	lose	lost	lost
burst	burst	burst	make	made	made
buy	bought	bought	put	put	put
catch	caught	caught	ride	rode	ridden
choose	chose	chosen	ring	rang	rung
come	came	come	rise	rose	risen
cost	cost	cost	run	ran	run
cut	cut	cut	say	said	said
dive	dove, dived	dived	see	saw	seen
			set	set	set
do	did	done	shake	shook	shaken
draw	drew	drawn	shine	shone	shone
drink	drank	drunk	shrink	shrank	shrunk
drive	drove	driven	shut	shut	shut
eat	ate	eaten	sing	sang	sung
fall	fell	fallen	sink	sank	sunk
fight	fought	fought	sit	sat	sat
fly	flew	flown	speak	spoke	spoken
freeze	froze	frozen	spring	sprang	sprung
get	got	gotten	steal	stole	stolen
give	gave	given	swim	swam	swum
go	went	gone	swing	swung	swung
grow	grew	grown	take	took	taken
hang	hung	hung	teach	taught	taught
hear	heard	heard	tear	tore	torn
hide	hid	hidden, hid	throw	threw	thrown
hit	hit	hit	wake	woke, waked	woken, awakened
hurt	hurt	hurt	wear	wore	worn
keep	kept	kept	weave	wove	woven
know	knew	known	write	wrote	written

Commonly Misused Words

Below is a list of commonly misused words. These words sound the same or similar or are often confused with each other. Read through each set of words and their meanings. Then read the examples. If you are ever unsure about which word to use, consult a dictionary.

accept, except
I accept your offer to work here.
I have everything I need except for the green paint.

a lot
Mike hopes to make a lot of money in his new job.

already, all ready
I already took my weekly spelling test.
I'm all ready to go to dinner.

bare, bear
It's too cold to walk around in bare feet.
A bear sleeps in winter.

blew, blue
The wind blew gently.
The sky was clear blue.

by, buy
The plane whizzed by overhead.
Alton wants to buy a new coat for winter.

can, may
Can Shane win the pie-eating contest?
May I go to the carnival on Saturday?

cent, scent, sent
A penny is worth one cent.
The flower shop had a strong scent.
My dad sent my mom flowers.

chose, choose
Antonia chose to walk home from school.
They often choose to walk home from school.

close, clothes
Close the door, please.
Grandpa has worn the same clothes since 1977.

creak, creek
Old and worn floors sometimes creak when you walk on them.
The water in the creek flows quietly.

dear, deer
I hold my friends dear to my heart.
Deer are shy animals.

desert, dessert
The desert is dry and hot.
Rodrigo always saves room for dessert.

dew, do, due
I love the feel of morning dew on my bare feet.
Bart forgot to do his chores last night.
Homework is always due at the beginning of class.

doesn't, don't
Huang doesn't like boxing.
I don't, either.

eye, I
I poked myself in the eye.
I have perfect vision.

fewer, less
Hank has fewer baseball cards than Joseph.
Hank has less time to collect baseball cards.

fir, fur
Fir trees are evergreen trees.
Many people don't like the idea of fur coats.

for, four
I'm excited for you.
Jamie's little brother is four years old.

good, well
Have a good day.
Our team played well.

hare, hair
A hare looks like a big rabbit.
Dad is losing his hair with age.

heal, heel
That cut should heal soon.
Sammy injured the heel of his foot.

hear, here
It's hard to hear the TV when the buses go by outside.
Most of the time it's quiet in here.

hi, high
Don't forget to say hi to the coach for me.
The flag is flying high.

hole, whole
A bagel has a hole in the middle.
I always eat the whole bagel for breakfast.

hour, our
Mom takes a yoga class for an hour on Wednesday nights.
Our family believes that exercise is important.

Commonly Misused Words

its, it's
The cat licked its paws.
It's a very cute kitten.

knew, new
Kim knew all of the answers on the game show.
She bought a new dress for the occasion.

knight, night
Fairy tales often involve a knight in shining armor.
The stars shine brightly at night.

knot, not
Sailors know how to make and undo every kind of knot.
I am not very good with my hands.

knows, nose
My teacher knows a lot about the planet Mars.
Margo has freckles on her nose.

lay, lie
Lay the pillow on the bed.
Lie down and take a nap.

lead, led
It's important to make sure there isn't any lead in the water.
The mayor led the city parade.

loose, lose
My shoelaces came loose in gym.
I thought for sure that I would lose.

mail, male
The mail is delivered six days a week.
A male is a man.

main, Maine, mane
My main concern is that I'll miss my flight.
The state of Maine is famous for its delicious blueberries.
A horse has a mane of hair on its neck.

meat, meet
Vegetarians don't eat meat.
My friends and I meet every Sunday morning for breakfast.

oar, or, ore
Use an oar to row the boat.
We can take a speedboat or a sailboat.
Ore is a mineral that contains metal.

one, won
Liza's family has one car.
Elizabeth won the race for class president.

pain, pane
I was in pain after the book fell on my foot.
The window pane needed to be washed.

pair, pare, pear
Ted wore his new pair of cowboy boots.
To pare an apple means to peel it.
I usually eat a juicy pear for dessert.

passed, past
Roberto had already passed several gas stations.
It's best to think ahead and not dwell on the past.

peace, piece
Many politicians speak of working toward world peace.
Joy asked for a small piece of pumpkin pie.

plain, plane
Jan wore a plain dress to her wedding.
As a result of bad weather, the plane took off an hour late.

pore, pour, poor
A pore is a tiny opening in the skin.
Would you pour the milk, please?
I felt poor after I spent my allowance.

read, red
I read the book in just one sitting.
Damien has bright red hair.

right, write
Is this the right place to sign up for the karate class?
Did you write a thank-you letter to Grandpa?

road, rode, rowed
The road was dusty and rocky.
We rode horses around the corral.
Sumi rowed the boat to shore.

sea, see
Adrian has always liked the salty air by the sea.
Alma can't see very well without her glasses.

seam, seem
The seam in Melvin's shirt was unraveling.
He didn't seem to care, though.

sew, so, sow
My mom taught me how to sew when I was just ten years old.
Her car had a flat tire, so she was late.
A gardener must sow seeds to grow plants.

Commonly Misused Words

sit, set
May I sit down next to you?
Latoya carefully set her tea on the glass table.

some, sum
Priya sold some of her old sweaters to earn extra money.
The sum of 10 and 10 is 20.

son, sun
I'd like to have both a son and a daughter.
The sun finally came out from behind the clouds.

stationery, stationary
Fiona writes letters on fancy stationery.
My stationary bike doesn't go anywhere when I pedal.

tail, tale
The dog wagged its tail excitedly.
Javier likes to tell tales about his family.

than, then
I'm taller than you.
Let's go shopping and then go to lunch.

their, there, they're
Yvonne and her sister went to visit their grandparents.
Juan likes to go over there because the kids have a lot of toys.
I think they're nice people.

threw, through
The pitcher threw the ball hard and fast.
The dog jumped through hoops at the circus.

to, too, two
Dad dislikes going to the dentist.
I am too tired to cook dinner for the family tonight.
Drake has two younger sisters.

waist, waste
Niles complains that his waist is getting too big.
Pierre doesn't like to waste too much of his time.

wait, weight
Julio is impatient and refuses to wait for anyone.
It's hard to lose weight if you don't exercise.

wear, where
Ruthie likes to wear large hoop earrings every day.
Do you know where the Rocky Mountains are?

which, witch
Which dress should I wear to the concert?
Zoe dressed as a witch for Halloween.

who's, whose
Who's going to take me to my swim meet?
Whose goggles are these?

wood, would
The burning wood in the fireplace smelled good.
Would you mind turning up the heat?

you're, your
You're going to get into trouble for skipping school.
Your dad will be very upset.

Answer Key

A. 1. H   2. A   3. S   4. S

B. lock

C. 1. C   2. P   3. S   4. S

D. 1. they will   2. we have

E. unhappy

F. 2 should be circled.

G. The words in bold should be circled.
1. IM; (You); **wait**   3. E; I, **burned**
2. IN; you, **do believe**   4. D; article, **made**

H. 1. CP
    2. CS

I. 1. I   2. RO   3. CS

J. [After I moved into town], <u>I rented a beautiful new</u>
         DO
    <u>apartment</u>.

Check What You Know (P. 2)

K. The words in bold should be circled.

    Ms. Chang rounded up the <u>group</u> and began the <u>tour</u> of the **Jefferson Memorial**.

L. The words in bold should be circled.

    My favorite <u>uncle</u>, **Tom Fiske**, was recently elected mayor of Greenville.

M. 1. past   2. future   3. present   4. future

N. 1. are; go   3. learn; take
    2. sat; laid   4. Set; sitting

O. 2 should be circled.

P. The words in bold should be circled.
1. IP; **Nobody**   3. PP; **its**
2. OP; **him**   4. SP; **He**

Q. The words in bold should be circled.

    Janet and Jason met to discuss the response to <u>their</u> request.

R. 1. adjective   4. adjective
    2. adverb   5. adjective
    3. adjective   6. adverb

S. The words in bold should be circled.

    I don't have the time <u>or</u> the patience to talk **about** <u>the complaints</u> **of** <u>those people</u>.

Check What You Know (P. 3)

T.
        956 E. Garden Circle
        Bowman, TX 78787
        April 13, 2005

Dear Steve,

    We're so excited you're coming to visit! Even little Scott managed to say, "Uncle Steve visit," which was pretty good for a child of only twenty-two months, wouldn't you agree? Oh, I want to be sure I have the information correct. Please let me know as soon as possible if any of this is wrong: flight 561, arrives at 3:10 P.M., May 22, 2005. See you then.

        Your sister,
        Amanda

Unit 1 Vocabulary

Lesson 1, Synonyms and Antonyms (P. 5)

A. Answers will vary.

B. Sentences will vary.

C. Answers may vary. Possible answers are given.
1. success   5. none   9. enemy
2. present   6. remember   10. never
3. after   7. hate   11. dark
4. fast   8. yes   12. backward

D. Answers may vary. Possible answers are given.
1. rough   3. build
2. begin   4. remember

Lesson 2, Homonyms (P. 6)

A. 1. weight   9. mist   15. meets
    2. sail   10. see   16. rein
    3. browse   11. threw;   17. brake
    4. days; inn   through   18. There
    5. floe   12. buy;   19. flew;
    6. boulder   beach   straight
    7. pier   13. aisle   20. allowed
    8. loan   14. principal

B. 1. way
   2. steel
   3. sale
   4. fair
   5. made
   6. dear
   7. eight
   8. vein or vane
   9. straight
   10. through
   11. sore
   12. board
   13. sea
   14. cent or scent
   15. pair or pear
   16. piece
   17. son
   18. blew

Lesson 3, Homographs (P. 7)

A. 1. b   3. a
   2. b   4. b

B. 1. checkers   3. can
   2. duck   4. alight

C. 1. stall   4. quack
   2. snap   5. punch
   3. squash

Lesson 4, Prefixes (P. 8)

A. 1. impractical; not practical
   2. misbehave; behave badly
   3. uneasy; not at ease
   4. nonviolent; not violent
   5. unusual; not usual or expected

B. 1. un-; not expected
   2. dis-; not appear or opposite of appear
   3. dis-; not agree
   4. mis-; spell a name wrong
   5. pre-; see before anyone else
   6. re-; to enter again
   7. mis-; put in the wrong place
   8. im-; not possible
   9. non-; not making stops
   10. un-; not important
   11. in-; not sane
   12. pre-; to judge beforehand

Lesson 5, Suffixes (P. 9)

A. 1. mountainous; full of mountains
   2. helpful; full of help
   3. snowy; full of snow
   4. national; related to a nation
   5. knowledgeable; inclined to have knowledge of

B. 1. -able; able to be broken
   2. -less; without end
   3. -ous; full of hazards
   4. -able; able to be inflated, suitable for inflating
   5. -ous; full of poison
   6. -able; able to be depended on
   7. -ous; full of humor
   8. -ful; full of tears
   9. -y; full of bumps
   10. -less; without care
   11. -al; relating to nature
   12. -al; relating to magic

Lesson 6, Contractions (P. 10)

A. 1. they're; they are
   2. won't; will not
   3. There's; There is
   4. That's; That is
   shouldn't; should not
   5. weren't; were not
   6. doesn't; does not
   7. can't; cannot
   it's; it is
   8. they've; they have
   they'll; they will
   9. It's; It is
   aren't; are not
   10. they'd; they would

B. 1. I have; I've
   I would, I'd
   2. It is; It's
   what is; what's
   3. I will; I'll
   4. does not; doesn't

Lesson 7, Compound Words (P. 11)

A. Answers will vary. Possible compound words include: air-condition, airline, airport, blackberry, blackbird, doorknob, doorway, sandpaper, seabird, seaport, understand, underground, underline, undersea.

B. 1. water that moves quickly in a circle
   2. very deep, loose, wet sand that moves rapidly
   3. a snake that makes a rattling sound
   4. a small, circular band worn on the ear
   5. a group of people who ride together in a car
   6. a string or cord that secures a shoe to a foot

Lesson 8, Connotation/Denotation (P. 12)

A. 1. - ; +   5. + ; +   9. N; +
   2. + ; -   6. + ; N   10. - ; +
   3. - ; +   7. N; +   11. - ; N
   4. + ; -   8. + ; -   12. - ; +

B. Paragraphs will vary. Sample paragraph follows:

Jason <u>made</u> his way through the <u>group</u> of people. He <u>walked</u> through the doorway and <u>leaned</u> against the wall. His clothes were quite <u>colorful</u>. He <u>looked</u> at everyone with <u>friendly</u> eyes. Then he <u>laughed</u> and said in a <u>pleasant</u> tone, "I'm finally here."

Lesson 9, Idioms (P. 13)

A. 1. J   **4.** B or D   **7.** D or A   **10.** I
   2. C   **5.** K   **8.** H
   3. A or D   **6.** F   **9.** E; G

B. Answers will vary. Possible answers include:

1. undecided
2. very happy
3. in some type of trouble
4. very strange or peculiar
5. talk seriously
6. in trouble
7. very attentive
8. was found
9. worked together

Review (P. 14)

A. 1. A   **4.** A   **7.** A   **10.** S
   2. S   **5.** A   **8.** A   **11.** A
   3. S   **6.** S   **9.** S   **12.** A

B. 1. weak, week   **4.** read, red
   2. write, right   **5.** pain, pane
   3. blew, blue

C. 1. b   **3.** a
   2. b   **4.** b

D. 1. thankful   **5.** blacken
   2. repay   **6.** thankless
   3. disagree   **7.** unhappy
   4. foolish   **8.** mistake

Review (P. 15)

E. 1. does not; doesn't   **5.** must not; mustn't
   2. She would; She'd   **6.** Who is; Who's
   3. It is; It's   **7.** did not; didn't
   4. does not; doesn't

F. 1. doorknob   **4.** sidewalk
   2. footstool   **5.** greenhouse
   3. roadblock

G. 1. -   **4.** -   **7.** -   **10.** -
   2. +   **5.** +   **8.** -
   3. -   **6.** -   **9.** +

H. 1. hit the high spots; talk about the most important points
   2. cut corners; do something in the least expensive way
   3. pull some strings; use influence to gain something

Using What You've Learned (P. 16)

A. Sentences will vary.

B. Sentences may vary. Possible sentences include:

1. After the storm hit, the sky got lighter.

2. White clouds drifted across the morning sky.

3. The light wind was blowing leaves under the trees.

C. Sentences will vary but should include the following words:

   1. knew   **3.** chews   **5.** waste
   2. greater   **4.** wait

D. Sentences will vary.

Using What You've Learned (P. 17)

E. Answers will vary. Possible answers include:

   1. misplace   **6.** tireless
   2. indirect   **7.** remarkable
   3. useful, useless   **8.** misspell
   4. measurable   **9.** repay
   5. speechless   **10.** refund

F. Sentences will vary.

G. Answers will vary. Suggested answers:

   1. soggy; moist   **6.** rags; apparel
   2. holler; call   **7.** beg; request
   3. skinny; slender   **8.** chore; job
   4. ancient; antique   **9.** hack; carve
   5. gab; discuss   **10.** devour; dine

Unit 2   Sentences

Lesson 10, Recognizing Sentences (P. 18)

Items 2, 5, 7, 9, 10, 11, 12, 13, 16, 19, 20, 21, 22, 24, 28, and 29 are sentences. Each sentence should end with a period.

Lesson 11, Types of Sentences (P. 19)

   1. D; .   **9.** IM; .   **17.** IN; ?
   2. IM, .   **10.** E; !   **18.** IM; .
   3. IN; ?   **11.** IM; .   **19.** IN; ?
   4. IM; .   **12.** IN; ?   **20.** E; ! or IM; .
   5. IN; ?   **13.** IN; ?   **21.** D; .
   6. IN; ?   **14.** D; .   **22.** IN; ?
   7. D; . or E; !   **15.** IN; ?   **23.** IM; .
   8. IN; ?   **16.** IM; .

Lesson 12, Complete Subjects and Predicates (P. 20)

1. Bees/fly.
2. Trains/whistle.
3. A talented artist/drew this cartoon.
4. The wind/blew furiously.
5. My grandmother/made this dress last year.
6. We/surely have enjoyed the holiday.
7. These cookies/are made with rice.
8. This letter/came to the post office box.
9. They/rent a cabin in Colorado every summer.

10. Jennifer/is reading about the pioneer days in the West.
11. Our baseball team/won the third game of the series.
12. The band/played a cheerful tune.
13. A cloudless sky/is a great help to a pilot.
14. The voice of the auctioneer/was heard throughout the hall.
15. A sudden flash of lightning/startled us.
16. The wind/howled down the chimney.
17. Paul's dog/followed him to the grocery store.
18. Their apartment/is on the sixth floor.
19. We/have studied many interesting places.
20. Each player on the team/deserves credit for the victory.
21. Forest rangers/fought the raging fire.
22. A friend/taught Robert a valuable lesson.
23. Millions of stars/make up the Milky Way.
24. The airplane/was lost in the thick clouds.
25. Many of the children/waded in the pool.
26. Yellowstone Park/is a large national park.
27. Cold weather/is predicted for tomorrow.
28. The trees/were covered with moss.

Lesson 12, Complete Subjects and Predicates (P. 21)

B. Sentences will vary.

C. Sentences will vary.

Lesson 13, Simple Subjects and Predicates (P. 22)

1. A sudden <u>clap</u> of thunder/<u>frightened</u> all of us.
2. The soft <u>snow</u>/<u>covered</u> the fields and roads.
3. <u>We</u>/<u>drove</u> very slowly over the narrow bridge.
4. The <u>students</u>/<u>are making</u> an aquarium.
5. Our <u>class</u>/<u>read</u> about the founder of Hull House.
6. The <u>women</u>/<u>were talking</u> in the park.
7. This <u>album</u>/<u>has</u> many folk songs.
8. <u>We</u>/<u>are furnishing</u> the sandwiches for tonight's picnic.
9. All the <u>trees</u> on that lawn/<u>are</u> giant oaks.
10. Many <u>Americans</u>/<u>are working</u> in foreign countries.
11. The <u>manager</u>/<u>read</u> the names of the contest winners.
12. <u>Bill</u>/<u>brought</u> these large melons.
13. <u>We</u>/<u>opened</u> the front door of the house.
14. The two <u>mechanics</u>/<u>worked</u> on the car for an hour.
15. Black and yellow <u>butterflies</u>/<u>fluttered</u> among the flowers.
16. The <u>child</u>/<u>spoke</u> politely.
17. <u>We</u>/<u>found</u> many beautiful shells along the shore.
18. The best <u>part</u> of the program/<u>is</u> the dance number.

19. Every ambitious <u>person</u>/<u>is working</u> hard.
20. <u>Sheryl</u>/<u>swam</u> across the lake two times.
21. Our <u>program</u>/<u>will begin</u> promptly at eight o'clock.
22. The <u>handle</u> of this basket/<u>is</u> broken.
23. The <u>clock</u> in the tower/<u>strikes</u> every hour.
24. The white <u>farmhouse</u> on that road/<u>belongs</u> to my cousin.
25. The first <u>game</u> of the season/<u>will be played</u> tomorrow.

Lesson 14, Position of Subjects (P. 23)

1. The <u>movie</u> <u>is playing</u> when?
2. <u>I</u> <u>will</u> never <u>forget</u> my first train trip.
3. The <u>picture</u> I want to buy <u>is</u> here.
4. <u>He</u> <u>has</u> seldom <u>been</u> ill.
5. The <u>lights</u> <u>went</u> out.
6. <u>Bookcases</u> <u>were</u> on all sides of the room.
7. <u>You</u> <u>take</u> the roast from the oven.
8. The speeding <u>car</u> <u>swerved</u> around the sharp curve.
9. <u>You</u> <u>get</u> out of the swimming pool.
10. <u>You</u> <u>study</u> for the spelling test.
11. Two <u>children</u> <u>are</u> in the pool.

Lesson 15, Compound Subjects (P. 24)

A. 1. CS; Arturo and I/often work late on Friday.
2. SS; Sandy/left the person near the crowded exit.
3. CS; She and I/will mail the packages to San Francisco, California, today.
4. CS; Shanghai and New Delhi/are two cities visited by the group.
5. SS; The fire/spread rapidly to other buildings in the neighborhood.
6. CS; Luis and Lenora/helped their parents with the chores.
7. CS; Swimming, jogging, and hiking/were our favorite sports.
8. CS; Melbourne and Sydney/are important Australian cities.
9. CS; Eric and I/had an interesting experience Saturday.
10. CS; The Red Sea and the Mediterranean Sea/are connected by the Suez Canal.
11. CS; The Republicans and the Democrats/made many speeches before the election.
12. SS; The people/waved to us from the top of the cliff.
13. CS; Liz and Jim/crated the freshly-picked apples.
14. CS; Clean clothes and a neat appearance/are important in an interview.
15. CS; The kitten and the old dog/are good friends.

16. CS; David and Paul/are on their way to the swimming pool.
17. SS; Tom/combed his dog's shiny black coat.
18. CS; Redbud and dogwood trees/bloom in the spring.
19. SS; I/hummed a cheerful tune on the way to the meeting.
20. CS; Buffalo, deer, and antelope/once roamed the plains of North America.
21. CS; Gina and Hiroshi/raked the leaves.
22. CS; Brasília and São Paulo/are two cities in Brazil.
23. SS; Hang gliding/is a popular sport in Hawaii.
24. SS; Our class/went on a field trip to the aquarium.
25. SS; The doctor/asked him to get a blood test.

B. Sentences will vary.

Lesson 16, Compound Predicates (P. 25)

A. 1. CP; Edward/grinned and nodded.
 2. SP; Plants/need air to live.
 3. SP; Old silver tea kettles/were among their possessions.
 4. CP; My sister/buys and sells real estate.
 5. SP; Snow/covered every highway in the area.
 6. CP; Mr. Sanders/designs and makes odd pieces of furniture.
 7. SP; Popcorn/is one of my favorite snack foods.
 8. SP; Soccer/is one of my favorite sports.
 9. CP; The ducks/quickly crossed the road and found the ducklings.
 10. CP; They/came early and stayed late.
 11. SP; Crystal/participated in the Special Olympics this year.
 12. CP; José/raked and sacked the leaves.
 13. CP; Perry/built the fire and cooked supper.
 14. SP; We/collected old newspapers for the recycling center.
 15. SP; Doug/arrived in Toronto, Ontario, during the afternoon.
 16. SP; Tony's parents/are visiting in Oregon and Washington.
 17. SP; The Garzas/live in that apartment building on Oak Street.
 18. CP; The shingles/were picked up and delivered today.
 19. CP; The audience/talked and laughed before the performance.
 20. CP; Automobiles/crowd and jam that highway early in the morning.
 21. SP; The apples/are rotting in the boxes.
 22. CP; The leader of the group/grumbled and scolded.
 23. CP; She/worked hard and waited patiently.

24. SP; Nelson Mandela/is a great civil rights activist.
25. SP; The supervisor/has completed the work for the week.

B. Sentences will vary.

Lesson 17, Combining Sentences (P. 26)

 1. <u>Lightning and thunder</u> are part of a thunderstorm.
 2. Thunderstorms <u>usually happen in the spring and bring heavy rains.</u>
 3. Depending on how close or far away it is, <u>thunder sounds like a sharp crack or rumbles.</u>
 4. Lightning <u>is very exciting to watch but can be very dangerous.</u>
 5. Lightning <u>causes many fires and harms many people.</u>
 6. <u>An open field or a golf course</u> is an unsafe place to be during a thunderstorm.
 7. Benjamin Franklin <u>wanted to protect people from lightning and invented the lightning rod.</u>
 8. A lightning rod <u>is a metal rod placed on the top of a building and connected to the ground by a cable.</u>

Lesson 18, Direct Objects (P. 27)

 1. Juanita's good driving <u>prevented</u> an accident. [DO over "prevented"]
 2. Every person <u>should have</u> an appreciation of music. [DO over "should have"]
 3. Gene, <u>pass</u> the potatoes, please. [DO over "pass"]
 4. <u>Do</u> not <u>waste</u> your time on this project. [DO over "waste"]
 5. James, <u>did</u> you <u>keep</u> those coupons? [DO over "keep"]
 6. Geraldo <u>collects</u> foreign stamps. [DO over "collects"]
 7. Eli Whitney <u>invented</u> the cotton gin. [DO over "invented"]
 8. <u>Answer</u> my question. [DO over "Answer"]
 9. We <u>are picking</u> trophies for our bowling league. [DO over "are picking"]
 10. Who <u>invented</u> the steamboat? [DO over "invented"]
 11. I <u>am reading</u> Hemingway's *The Old Man and the Sea.* [DO over "am reading"]
 12. The North Star <u>guides</u> sailors. [DO over "guides"]

13. The Phoenicians <u>gave</u> the alphabet to ^{DO} civilization.

14. Every person <u>should study</u> world history. ^{DO}

15. Who <u>made</u> this cake? ^{DO}

16. <u>Can</u> you <u>find</u> a direct object in this sentence? ^{DO}

17. Who <u>wrote</u> the story of Johnny Tremain? ^{DO}

18. We <u>bought</u> several curios for our friends. ^{DO}

19. Tamara <u>read</u> the minutes of our last club ^{DO} meeting.

20. <u>Did</u> you ever <u>make</u> a time budget of your own? ^{DO}

21. Mountains <u>have</u> often <u>affected</u> the history of a ^{DO} nation.

22. Emma and Joe <u>baked</u> a pie. ^{DO}

Lesson 19, Indirect Objects (P. 28)

1. Certain marine plants <u>give</u> the Red Sea its color. ^{IO} ^{DO}

2. I <u>gave</u> the cashier a check for twenty dollars. ^{IO} ^{DO}

3. The magician <u>showed</u> the audience a few of her ^{IO} ^{DO} tricks.

4. The coach <u>taught</u> them the rules of the game. ^{IO} ^{DO}

5. Roberto <u>brought</u> us some foreign coins. ^{IO} ^{DO}

6. This interesting book <u>will give</u> every reader ^{IO} pleasure. ^{DO}

7. <u>Have</u> you <u>written</u> your brother a letter? ^{IO} ^{DO}

8. They <u>made</u> us some sandwiches to take on ^{IO} ^{DO} our hike.

9. The astronaut <u>gave</u> Mission Control the data. ^{IO} ^{DO}

10 I <u>bought</u> my friend an etching at the art exhibit. ^{IO} ^{DO}

11. James, <u>did</u> you <u>sell</u> Mike your car? ^{IO} ^{DO}

12. We <u>have given</u> the dog a thorough scrubbing. ^{IO} ^{DO}

13. <u>Give</u> the usher your ticket. ^{IO} ^{DO}

14. Carl <u>brought</u> my brother a gold ring from Mexico. ^{IO} ^{DO}

15. <u>Hand</u> me a pencil, please. ^{IO} ^{DO}

16. The conductor <u>gave</u> the orchestra a short break. ^{IO} ^{DO}

17. <u>Show</u> me the picture of your boat. ^{IO} ^{DO}

18. I <u>have given</u> you my money. ^{IO} ^{DO}

19. <u>Give</u> Lee this message. ^{IO} ^{DO}

20. The club <u>gave</u> the town a new statue. ^{IO} ^{DO}

Lesson 20, Independent and Subordinate Clauses (P. 29)

A. 1. <u>Frank will be busy</u> because he is studying.
   2. <u>I have only one hour</u> that I can spare.
   3. <u>The project must be finished</u> when I get back.
   4. <u>Gloria volunteered to do the typing</u> that needs to be done.
   5. <u>The work is going too slowly</u> for us to finish on time.
   6. Before Nathan started to help, <u>I didn't think we could finish</u>.
   7. <u>What else should we do</u> before we relax?
   8. Since you forgot to give this page to Gloria, <u>you can type it</u>.
   9. After she had finished typing, <u>we completed the project</u>.
   10. <u>We actually got it finished</u> before the deadline.

B. 1. The people <u>who went shopping</u> found a great sale.
   2. Tony's bike, <u>which is a mountain bike</u>, came from that store.
   3. Juana was sad <u>when the sale was over</u>.
   4. Marianne was excited <u>because she wanted some new things</u>.
   5. Thomas didn't find anything <u>since he went late</u>.
   6. The mall <u>where we went shopping</u> was new.
   7. The people <u>who own the stores</u> are proud of the beautiful setting.
   8. The mall, <u>which is miles away</u>, is serviced by the city bus.
   9. We ran as fast as we could <u>because the bus was coming</u>.
   10. We were panting <u>because we had run fast</u>.

Lesson 21, Adjective and Adverb Clauses (P. 30)

A. 1. adjective; whose bravery won many victories
2. adjective; who reads the most books
3. adverb; because he hadn't set the alarm
4. adverb; when our team comes off the field
5. adjective; that he hears
6. adjective; that we planned

B. Sentences will vary.

Lesson 22, Compound and Complex Sentences (P. 31)

A.
1. CP	7. CX	13. CX	19. CX
2. CP	8. CX	14. CX	20. CP
3. CX	9. CP	15. CP	21. CX
4. CP	10. CP	16. CP	22. CP
5. CX	11. CP	17. CX	23. CP
6. CP	12. CX	18. CX	24. CX

Lesson 22, Compound and Complex Sentences (P. 32)

B. 1. [The <u>streets</u> <u>are</u> filled with cars], but [the sidewalks <u>are</u> empty].
2. [Those <u>apples</u> <u>are</u> too sour to eat], but [those pears <u>are</u> perfect].
3. [<u>She</u> <u>studies</u> hard], but [<u>she</u> <u>saves</u> some time to enjoy herself].
4. [<u>They</u> <u>lost</u> track of time], so [<u>they</u> <u>were</u> late].
5. [<u>Eric</u> <u>had</u> not <u>studied</u>], so [<u>he</u> <u>failed</u> the test].
6. [Yesterday <u>it</u> <u>rained</u> all day], but [today the <u>sun</u> <u>is shining</u>].
7. [<u>I</u> <u>set</u> the alarm to get up early], but [<u>I</u> <u>couldn't</u> <u>get</u> up].
8. [<u>They</u> <u>may sing and dance</u> until dawn], but [<u>they</u> <u>will be</u> exhausted].
9. [My <u>friend</u> <u>moved</u> to Texas], and [<u>I</u> <u>will miss</u> her].
10. [<u>They</u> <u>arrived</u> at the theater early], but [there <u>was</u> still a long <u>line</u>].
11. [<u>Lisa</u> <u>took</u> her dog to the veterinarian], but [his office <u>was</u> closed].
12. [The black <u>cat</u> <u>leaped</u>], but [fortunately <u>it</u> <u>didn't</u> <u>catch</u> the bird].
13. [<u>I</u> <u>found</u> a baseball in the bushes], and [<u>I</u> <u>gave</u> it to my brother].
14. [<u>We</u> <u>loaded</u> the cart with groceries], and [<u>we</u> <u>went</u> to the checkout].
15. [The <u>stadium</u> <u>was showered</u> with lights], but [the stands <u>were</u> empty].
16. [The small <u>child</u> <u>whimpered</u>], and [her <u>mother</u> <u>hugged</u> her].
17. [The dark <u>clouds</u> <u>rolled</u> in], and [then <u>it</u> <u>began</u> to rain].

C. 1. The hummingbird is the only bird <u>that can fly backward</u>.
2. The cat <u>that is sitting in the window</u> is mine.
3. The car <u>that is parked outside</u> is new.

4. Jack, <u>who is a football star</u>, is class president.
5. Bonnie, <u>who is an artist</u>, is also studying computer science.
6. John likes food <u>that is cooked in the microwave</u>.
7. The composer <u>who wrote the music</u> comes from Germany.
8. We missed seeing him <u>because we were late</u>.
9. <u>When Jake arrives</u>, we will tell him <u>what happened</u>.
10. She walked slowly <u>because she had hurt her leg</u>.
11. <u>When she walked to the podium</u>, everyone applauded.
12. <u>If animals could talk</u>, they might have a lot to tell.
13. Many roads <u>that were built in our city</u> are no longer traveled.
14. My address book, <u>which is bright red</u>, is gone.
15. Ann, <u>who is from Georgia</u>, just started working here today.
16. The crowd cheered <u>when the player came to bat</u>.
17. <u>When he hit the ball</u>, everyone cheered.

Lesson 23, Correcting Run-on Sentences (P. 33)

Sentences will vary.

Lesson 24, Expanding Sentences (P. 34)

A. Sentences will vary.

B. Sentences will vary.

Review (P. 35)

A.
1. IN; ?	3. X	6. IN; ?	9. D; .
2. E; ! or IM; .	4. D; .	7. E; !	10. IM; .
	5. E; !	8. X	

B. 1. <u>The lights around the public square</u> went out.
2. <u>Stations</u> are in all parts of our country.
3. Carmen collects <u>fans</u> for a hobby.
4. We <u>drove slowly across the bridge</u>.
5. We <u>saw</u> an unusual flower.
6. Taro <u>swims</u> and <u>dives</u> quite well.
7. The <u>cake</u> and <u>bread</u> are kept in the box.
8. The referee gave our <u>team</u> a fifteen-yard penalty.
9. A good citizen obeys the <u>laws</u>, but a bad citizen doesn't.
10. Please lend <u>me</u> your raincoat, so I can stay dry.

C.
1. CX	4. CP	7. CX	10. CP
2. CP	5. CX	8. CP	
3. CX	6. CX	9. CX	

Review (P. 36)

D. 1. The director <u>gave</u> the actors a new script.
   <small>IO</small>   <small>DO</small>
2. Jenny <u>showed</u> her friends her vacation slides.
   <small>IO</small>   <small>DO</small>

3. Ms. Lopez <u>took</u> her sick neighbor some chicken
   soup. [IO above "her sick neighbor", DO above "chicken soup"]

4. We <u>handed</u> the cashier our money. [IO above "the cashier", DO above "our money"]

5. Enrique, please <u>give</u> your brother his jacket. [IO above "your brother", DO above "his jacket"]

E. The words in bold should be circled.

   1. <u>The campers got wet</u> **when it started raining**.
   2. <u>The candidates</u> **that I voted for in the election** <u>won easily</u>.
   3. **Before the board voted on the issue**, <u>it held public hearings</u>.
   4. <u>The freeway through town is a road</u> **where vehicles often speed**.
   5. **While we waited**, <u>the children kept us entertained</u>.

F. 1. who are trained in weather forecasting; adjective clause
   2. before I decided on a college; adverb clause
   3. that I designed; adjective clause
   4. Although the furniture was old; adverb clause
   5. because they want to stay healthy; adverb clause
   6. before I left; adverb clause

G. 1. A large goldfish lay just below the surface.
   2. The baseball flew over the roof.

H. 1. Dogs are Erica's favorite animal, and cats are John's favorite animal.
   2. The water reflected the sun, so we put on our sunglasses.

Using What You've Learned (P. 37)

A. 1. D
   2. E
   3. A
   4. A
   5. A
   6. D; E
   7. B
   8. C
   9. We
   10. We
   11. Be at my house by seven o'clock

B. The words in bold should be circled.

   1. <u>The streamers sagged</u> **after we hung them**.
   2. <u>Mark knows party planning</u> **because he has many parties**.
   3. <u>Everyone</u> **who wants to go to the party** <u>must bring something</u>.
   4. **If everyone brings something**, <u>the party will be great</u>.
   5. **Unless I am wrong**, <u>the party is tomorrow</u>.
   6. **As if everything had been done**, <u>Jake ran out of the room</u>.

7. <u>The girls</u> **who planned the party** <u>received roses</u>.
8. <u>I will never forget the day</u> **that I fell on my face at a party**.

C. Sentences will vary.

Using What You've Learned (P. 38)

D. 1. The news of the storm was reported on a television bulletin.
   2. The small airplane taxied into the hangar.
   3. The tired passengers came down the ramp.

E. Sentences will vary.

F.   In space medicine research, new types of miniature equipment for checking how the body functions have been developed. On the spacecraft, astronauts' breathing rates, heartbeats, and blood pressure are taken with miniature devices no larger than a pill. These devices detect the information and transmit it to scientists back on Earth. They allow the scientists to monitor astronauts' body responses from a long distance and over long periods of time.

G. Sentences will vary.

Unit 3   Grammar and Usage

Lesson 25, Common and Proper Nouns (P. 39)

A. 1. <u>Maria</u> is my <u>sister</u>. [P above Maria, C above sister]

   2. <u>Honolulu</u> is the chief <u>city</u> and <u>capital</u> of <u>Hawaii</u>. [P above Honolulu, C above city, C above capital, P above Hawaii]

   3. <u>Rainbow Natural Bridge</u> is hidden away in the wild mountainous <u>part</u> of southern <u>Utah</u>. [P above Rainbow Natural Bridge, C above part, P above Utah]

   4. The <u>Declaration of Independence</u> is often called the birth <u>certificate</u> of the <u>United States</u>. [P above Declaration of Independence, C above certificate, P above United States]

   5. <u>Abraham Lincoln</u>, <u>Edgar Allan Poe</u>, and <u>Frederic Chopin</u> were born in the same <u>year</u>. [P above each name, C above year]

B. Proper nouns will vary.

C. Sentences will vary.

Lesson 26, Concrete, Abstract, and Collective Nouns (P. 40)

1. abstract
2. abstract
3. collective
4. abstract
5. collective
6. concrete
7. collective
8. collective
9. concrete
10. collective
11. abstract
12. collective
13. abstract
14. concrete
15. collective
16. abstract
17. concrete
18. collective
19. concrete
20. abstract
21. collective
22. collective
23. concrete
24. abstract
25. collective
26. collective
27. concrete
28. abstract
29. collective
30. concrete
31. collective
32. abstract
33. collective
34. concrete
35. collective
36. abstract
37. concrete
38. concrete
39. abstract
40. concrete
41. abstract
42. abstract

Lesson 27, Singular and Plural Nouns (P. 41)

A.
1. brushes
2. lunches
3. countries
4. benches
5. earrings
6. calves
7. pianos
8. foxes
9. daisies
10. potatoes
11. dishes
12. stores

Lesson 27, Singular and Plural Nouns (P. 42)

B.
1. booklets
2. tomatoes
3. trucks
4. chefs
5. branches
6. toddlers
7. pennies
8. potatoes
9. pieces
10. doors
11. islands
12. countries
13. houses
14. garages
15. fish
16. watches
17. elves
18. desks
19. pans
20. sheep
21. gardens
22. ponies
23. solos
24. trees
25. lights
26. churches
27. cities
28. spoonfuls
29. vacations
30. homes

C.
1. Put the apples and oranges in the boxes.
2. Jan wrote five letters to her friends.
3. Those buildings each have four elevators.
4. Our families drove many miles to get to the lakes.
5. The tops of those cars were damaged in the storms.
6. My aunts and uncles attended the family reunion.

Lesson 28, Possessive Nouns (P. 43)

A.
1. girl's
2. child's
3. women's
4. children's
5. John's
6. baby's
7. boys'
8. teacher's
9. Dr. Ray's
10. ladies'
11. brother's
12. soldier's
13. men's
14. aunt's
15. Ms. Jones's

B.
1. Jim's cap
2. Kathy's wrench
3. baby's smile
4. my friend's car
5. Kim's new shoes
6. the dog's collar
7. Frank's golf clubs
8. the runners' shoes
9. our parents' friends
10. the editor's opinion
11. the children's lunches
12. Kyle's coat
13. the teacher's assignment

Lesson 29, Appositives (P. 44)

A. The words in bold should be circled.

1. **Banff**, the large Canadian national park, is my favorite place to visit.
2. The **painter** Vincent Van Gogh cut off part of his ear.
3. The **White House**, home of the President of the United States, is open to the public for tours.
4. **Uncle Marco**, my mother's brother, is an engineer.
5. **Earth**, the only inhabited planet in our solar system, is home to a diverse population of plants and animals.
6. The **scorpion**, a native of the southwestern part of North America, has a poisonous sting.
7. Emily's prize Persian **cat** Amelia won first prize at the cat show.
8. **Judge Andropov**, the presiding judge, sentenced the criminal to prison.
9. Paula's **friend** from Florida, Luisa, watched a space shuttle launch.

B. Answers will vary.

Lesson 30, Verbs (P. 45)

1. (is) scattering; scattered; (have, had, has) scattered
2. (is) expressing; expressed; (have, had, has) expressed
3. (is) painting; painted; (have, had, has) painted
4. (is) calling; called; (have, had, has) called
5. (is) cooking; cooked; (have, had, has) cooked
6. (is) observing; observed; (have, had, has) observed
7. (is) looking; looked; (have, had, has) looked
8. (is) walking; walked; (have, had, has) walked
9. (is) rambling; rambled; (have, had, has) rambled
10. (is) shouting; shouted; (have, had, has) shouted
11. (is) noticing; noticed; (have, had, has) noticed
12. (is) ordering; ordered; (have, had, has) ordered
13. (is) gazing; gazed; (have, had, has) gazed
14. (is) borrowing; borrowed; (have, had, has) borrowed
15. (is) starting; started; (have, had, has) started
16. (is) working; worked; (have, had, has) worked

Lesson 31, Verb Phrases (P. 46)

1. were held
2. invented
3. was
4. was
5. built
6. will arrive
7. was
8. has made
9. covered
10. have ridden
11. is molding
12. spent
13. are posted
14. has found
15. is going
16. have trimmed
17. exports
18. is reading
19. helped
20. was discovered
21. was called
22. are planning
23. has howled
24. have arrived
25. have written
26. can name
27. received
28. was printed
29. are working
30. was painted

Lesson 32, Verb Tenses (P. 47)

A. Answers will vary.

B.
1. future
2. past
3. future
4. present
5. past
6. past
7. present
8. future
9. past
10. past

Lesson 33, Present Perfect and Past Perfect Tenses (P. 48)

A.
1. past perfect
2. past perfect
3. present perfect
4. past perfect
5. present perfect
6. present perfect
7. present perfect
8. past perfect
9. present perfect
10. present perfect

B.
1. has
2. have
3. had
4. has
5. had
6. has
7. had

Lesson 34, Using *Is/Are* and *Was/Were* (P. 49)

A.
1. is
2. are
3. is
4. are
5. is
6. are
7. are
8. Are
9. is
10. are

B.
1. were
2. were
3. were
4. were
5. was
6. was
7. was
8. were
9. were
10. was

Lesson 35, Past Tenses of *See*, *Go*, and *Begin* (P. 50)

A.
1. saw
2. gone
3. began
4. went
5. begun
6. seen
7. gone
8. saw
9. seen
10. went
11. begun
12. began
13. gone
14. began
15. begun
16. saw
17. went
18. seen
19. went
20. began
21. began

B. Answers will vary.

Lesson 36, *Freeze*, *Choose*, *Speak*, and *Break* (P. 51)

A.
1. spoken
2. frozen
3. broke
4. spoken
5. chosen
6. broken
7. spoken
8. froze
9. chose
10. broken
11. spoke
12. froze
13. broken
14. chose
15. spoke
16. frozen

B.
1. frozen
2. broken
3. chosen
4. spoke
5. chosen
6. chose
7. broken
8. spoke
9. frozen
10. spoken

Lesson 37, *Come*, *Ring*, *Drink*, *Know*, and *Throw* (P. 52)

A.
1. drank
2. rung
3. drunk
4. knew
5. thrown
6. come
7. rang
8. known
9. threw
10. came
11. drunk
12. come
13. knew
14. thrown
15. come
16. rang
17. drank

B. Sentences will vary.

Lesson 38, Past Tenses of *Give*, *Take*, and *Write* (P. 53)

A.
1. took
2. taken
3. wrote
4. written
5. gave
6. given
7. written
8. written
9. given
10. wrote
11. taken
12. taken
13. gave
14. took
15. given
16. written
17. took
18. gave
19. written

B.
1. took
2 written
3. gave
4. given
5. taken
6. took
7. gave
8. taken

Lesson 39, *Eat*, *Fall*, *Draw*, *Drive*, and *Run* (P. 54)

A.
1. drawn
2. driven; began
3. fallen
4. eaten; ran
5. drew
6. run
7. fallen; ran
8. fallen
9. drove
10. eaten
11. ate
12. fallen
13. ran

B.
1. drove
2. drew
3. fallen
4. fell
5. driven
6. ran
7. ate
8. eaten
9. drawn
10. run

Lesson 40, Forms of *Do* (P. 55)

A.
1. doesn't
2. did
3. done
4. doesn't
5. did
6. Don't
7. done
8. Don't
9. doesn't
10. don't
11. done
12. did
13. Doesn't
14. Doesn't
15. done
16. doesn't

B. Sentences will vary.

C. Sentences will vary.

Lesson 41, Mood (P. 56)

1. imperative	**8.** subjunctive	**15.** indicative
2. indicative	**9.** imperative	**16.** indicative
3. subjunctive	**10.** subjunctive	**17.** subjunctive
4. imperative	**11.** imperative	**18.** imperative
5. indicative	**12.** imperative	**19.** subjunctive
6. indicative	**13.** indicative	
7. indicative	**14.** subjunctive	

Lesson 42, Transitive and Intransitive Verbs (P. 57)

A. 1. T; joined **6.** T; preferred **11.** I; swam
2. T; wanted **7.** T; liked **12.** T; was
3. I; exercised **8.** T; switched **13.** T; had
4. I; became **9.** T; took **14.** I; splashed
5. I; worked **10.** T; used

B. The words in bold should be circled.

1. Carlos <u>walked</u> **Tiny** every day.
2. Tiny usually <u>pulled</u> **Carlos** along.
3. Carlos <u>washed</u> **Tiny** every other week.
4. Tiny <u>loved</u> **water**.
5. He <u>splashed</u> **Carlos** whenever he could.
6. Tiny also <u>loved</u> rawhide **bones**.
7. He <u>chewed</u> the **bones** until they were gone.
8. Carlos <u>found</u> **Tiny** when Tiny was just a puppy.

Lesson 43, Active and Passive Voice (P. 58)

A. 1. A **4.** A **7.** P **10.** A
2. A **5.** P **8.** P
3. A **6.** A **9.** P

B. Sentences will vary.

C. Sentences will vary.

Lesson 44, Gerunds (P. 59)

1. living	**15.** Playing
2. fighting	**16.** Planning
3. Landing	**17.** packing
4. Climbing	**18.** howling
5. moaning	**19.** doing
6. barking	**20.** living
7. Keeping	**21.** planting; hunting;
8. hanging	fishing
9. Laughing	**22.** writing
10. Being	**23.** skating
11. Making	**24.** boating
12. Winning	**25.** Pressing
13. pitching	**26.** mapping
14. eating	**27.** Swimming
	28. driving

Lesson 45, Infinitives (P. 60)

1. to go	**16.** to enter
2. to see	**17.** to mail
3. to serve	**18.** To cook
4. To shoot	**19.** to meet
5. to walk	**20.** to speak
6. to stand; to sit; to walk; to dance	**21.** to exhibit
	22. To succeed
7. to use; to make	**23.** to see
8. to get	**24.** to eat
9. to make	**25.** to see
10. to clean	**26.** to have; to be
11. to be	**27.** to receive
12. to travel	**28.** To score
13. to play	**29.** to go
14. to rise	**30.** to paint
15. to see	

Lesson 46, Participles (P. 61)

1. running	**11.** produced	**21.** Teasing
2. showing	**12.** burdened	**22.** lifting
3. scampering	**13.** thinking	**23.** chirping
4. hidden	**14.** injured	**24.** surviving
5. advancing	**15.** expanding	**25.** dedicated
6. Biting	**16.** fanned	**26.** Homing
7. falling	**17.** shoving	**27.** whistling
8. whispering	**18.** frozen	**28.** Ironed
9. preparing	**19.** playing	**29.** standing
10. enjoying	**20.** cleaned	**30.** loving

Lesson 47, Using *May/Can* and *Teach/Learn* (P. 62)

A. 1. can **4.** can **7.** can **10.** May
2. can **5.** can **8.** can
3. may **6.** may **9.** can

B. 1. teach **4.** learn **7.** teach
2. learn **5.** teach **8.** teach;
3. teach **6.** teach learn

Lesson 48, Using *Sit/Set* and *Lay/Lie* (P. 63)

A. 1. sit **4.** set **7.** set **10.** sit
2. set **5.** Set **8.** sat
3. sit **6.** sits **9.** sit

B. 1. lay **4.** laid **7.** Lay **10.** lain
2. Lie **5.** lay **8.** laid
3. lies **6.** lie **9.** lie

Lesson 49, Pronouns (P. 64)

1. you; my
2. you; me; I; them
3. you; me; our
4. I; you
5. We; him
6. me
7. We; they; us
8. She; me
9. She; you; me; her
10. We; them
11. we; our
12. He; their
13. She; my
14. They; us; them
15. she
16. he; you
17. She; us
18. I
19. your
20. me
21. you; our
22. I; you; my; you; it
23. I; him; my; we; her
24. they; us; their
25. Your; your
26. us; her; our

Lesson 50, Demonstrative and Indefinite Pronouns (P. 65)

A.
1. Those
2. That
3. these
4. This; that
5. those
6. that
7. This
8. these
9. These
10. this
11. those
12. this
13. those
14. These
15. that
16. that

B.
1. Both
2. each
3. Several
4. some
5. Everyone
6. someone
7. Some
8. each
9. anyone
10. someone
11. Both
12. One
13. Each
14. Some
15. someone
16. Everybody

Lesson 51, Antecedents (P. 66)

The words in bold should be circled.

1. **Everyone**; his or her
2. **Each**; his or her
3. **Sophia**; her
4. **I**; my
5. **members**; their
6. **women**; their
7. **Someone**; her or his
8. **each**; his or her
9. **Joanne**; her
10. **woman**; her
11. **anyone**; his or her
12. **student**; his or her
13. **I**; my
14. **woman**; her
15. **one**; his or her
16. **Joseph**; his
17. **man**; his
18. **waiters**; their
19. **student**; his or her
20. **person**; her or his
21. **man**; his
22. **woman**; her
23. **Jeff and Tom**; their
24. **Cliff**; he
25. **bird**; its
26. **Mark**; his

Lesson 52, Relative Pronouns (P. 67)

The words in bold should be circled.

1. **letter**; that
2. **Karen**; who
3. **Robert Burns**; who
4. **Sylvia**; who
5. **shop**; that
6. **farmhouse**; that
7. **pearl**; that
8. **bridge**; which
9. **animal**; that
10. **regions**; that
11. **turkey**; that
12. **story**; which
13. **person**; whom
14. **hamburgers**; that
15. **Food**; that
16. **painting**; that
17. **sweater**; that
18. **one**; whom
19. **money**; that
20. **person**; who
21. **animal**; that
22. **guests**; whom
23. **file**; which
24. **artist**; whose
25. **attraction**; that
26. **writer**; whom

Lesson 53, Using *Who/Whom* (P. 68)

1. Who
2. Who
3. Whom
4. Who
5. Who
6. Who
7. Whom
8. Whom
9. Whom
10. Whom
11. Who
12. Whom
13. Who
14. Who
15. Whom
16. Who
17. Who
18. Whom
19. Who
20. Whom
21. Who

Lesson 54, Adjectives (P. 69)

A. Answers will vary.

B.
1. This; old; comfortable
2. a; funny
3. This; heavy; many; dangerous
4. The; eager; odd; every
5. The; tired; thirsty
6. favorite
7. The; solitary; the; lonely
8. the; sixth
9. These; damp
10. French
11. those
12. A; red; the; tall
13. The; heavy
14. A; tour; the
15. The; gorgeous; Italian
16. fresh
17. mashed; baked
18. Chinese

Lesson 55, Demonstrative Adjectives (P. 70)

1. those
2. That
3. those
4. those
5. That
6. Those
7. those
8. those
9. these
10. those
11. these
12. these
13. those
14. this
15. Those
16. these
17. those
18. That
19. These
20. those
21. these
22. these
23. These
24. those
25. Those

Lesson 56, Comparing with Adjectives (P. 71)

1. more changeable
2. most faithful
3. more agreeable
4. busiest
5. longer
6. loveliest
7. freshest
8. higher
9. more enjoyable
10. most reckless
11. youngest
12. tallest
13. more difficult
14. quietest

Lesson 57, Adverbs (P. 72)

A. 1. slowly; clearly; expressively
2. too; recklessly
3. slowly; quickly
4. too; harshly
5. here
6. everywhere
7. suddenly; quickly; around
8. too; rapidly
9. well
10. soundly
11. noisily
12. early
13. severely
14. quickly; steadily

B. Answers will vary.

Lesson 58, Comparing with Adverbs (P. 73)

A. 1. sooner
2. soonest
3. hard
4. more
5. faster
6. most

B. 1. fastest
2. faster
3. more seriously
4. the most frequently
5. more quickly
6. the most promptly
7. more promptly
8. the most eagerly
9. more carefully
10. hardest

Lesson 59, Using Adjectives and Adverbs (P. 74)

1. carefully
2. calm
3. furiously
4. patiently
5. cheerfully
6. well
7. promptly
8. respectfully
9. happy
10. legibly
11. slowly
12. happily
13. surely
14. well
15. easily
16. loudly
17. brightly
18. well
19. quickly
20. suddenly
21. cautiously
22. accurately
23. furiously
24. new
25. steadily
26. beautiful
27. courteously
28. well
29. well
30. really
31. foolishly
32. foolish
33. loudly
34. rapidly

Lesson 60, Prepositions (P. 75)

1. on
2. from; with
3. through; toward
4. between
5. for
6. about
7. into
8. to
9. across
10. against
11. over; into
12. across
13. among; of
14. beside
15. across; toward
16. behind
17. around
18. on
19. about; in
20. over; in
21. to
22. into
23. across
24. of; from
25. among
26. After; to
27. of; in

Lesson 61, Prepositional Phrases (P. 76)

The words in bold should be circled.

1. The airplane was flying (<u>above</u> the **clouds**).
2. We are moving (<u>to</u> **North Carolina**).
3. Sandra lives (<u>on</u> the second **block**).
4. An old water tower once stood (<u>on</u> that **hill**).
5. The car slid (<u>on</u> the wet **pavement**).
6. Sealing wax was invented (<u>in</u> the seventeenth **century**).
7. Motto rings were first used (<u>by</u> the **Romans**).
8. Tungsten, a metal, was discovered (<u>in</u> **1781**).
9. Roses originally came (<u>from</u> **Asia**).
10. The ball rolled (<u>into</u> the **street**).
11. Do you always keep the puppies (<u>in</u> a **pen**)?
12. The children climbed (<u>over</u> the **fence**).
13. She lives (<u>in</u> **Denver, Colorado**).
14 Columbus made three trips (<u>to</u> **North America**).
15. They spread the lunch (<u>under</u> the **shade**) (<u>of</u> the giant elm **tree**).
16. The treasure was found (<u>by</u> a scuba **diver**).
17. A squad (<u>of</u> **soldiers**) marched (<u>behind</u> the **tank**).
18. Shall I row (<u>across</u> the **stream**)?
19. Large airplanes fly (<u>across</u> the **nation**).
20. Walter looked (<u>into</u> the **sack**).
21. The cat ran (<u>up</u> the **pole**).
22. We visited the Alexander Graham Bell Museum (<u>in</u> **Nova Scotia**).
23. Many tourists come (<u>to</u> our **region**).
24. We spent last summer (<u>in</u> the **Adirondack Mountains**).
25. Do not stand (<u>behind</u> a parked **car**).

Lesson 62, Prepositional Phrases as Adjectives and Adverbs (P. 77)

1. They went <u>to the ranch</u>. *(adv.)*
2. The first savings bank was established <u>in France</u>. *(adv.)*
3. Fall Creek Falls <u>in Tennessee</u> is my home. *(adj.)*
4. Return all books <u>to the public library</u>. *(adv.)*
5. Mark lives <u>in an old house</u>. *(adv.)*
6. Tanya bought a sweater <u>with red trim</u>. *(adj.)*
7. The birds <u>in the zoo</u> are magnificent. *(adj.)*
8. Jade is found <u>in Burma</u>. *(adv.)*
9. I spent the remainder <u>of my money</u>. *(adj.)*
10. The magician waved a wand <u>over the hat</u>, and a rabbit appeared. *(adv.)*
11. The diameter <u>of a Sequoia tree trunk</u> can reach ten feet. *(adj.)*
12. The capital <u>of New York</u> is Albany. *(adj.)*
13. The narrowest streets are <u>near the docks</u>. *(adv.)*
14. Our family went <u>to the movie</u>. *(adv.)*
15. Roald Amundsen discovered the South Pole <u>in 1911</u>. *(adv.)*
16. The floor <u>in this room</u> is painted black. *(adj.)*
17. The dead leaves are blowing <u>across the yard</u>. *(adv.)*
18. A forest <u>of petrified wood</u> has been found. *(adj.)*
19. The mole's tunnel runs <u>across the lawn</u>. *(adv.)*

Lesson 63, Conjunctions (P. 78)

1. and
2. whereas
3. since
4. but
5. not only…but also
6. Neither…nor
7. and
8. Neither…nor
9. neither…nor
10. and
11. Either…or
12. and
13. Neither…nor
14. Although
15. when
16. since
17. while
18. Unless
19. although
20. Both…and
21. both…and
22. Unless
23. Neither…nor
24. while
25. when
26. Either…or
27. because

Lesson 64, Double Negatives (P. 79)

1. anything
2. anything
3. any
4. anything
5. any
6. any
7. anyone
8. any
9. any
10. any
11. anything
12. anything
13. any
14. any
15. anybody
16. any
17. any
18. anything
19. any
20. any
21. anything
22. any
23. any
24. any
25. any
26. anyone
27. anybody
28. anyone
29. any

Review (P. 80)

A. 1. adj.; n.; v.; prep.; n.
2. adj.; adj.; n.
3. adj.; n.; adv.; v.
4. n.; pron.; prep.; pron.; n.
5. n.; prep.; pron.; n.
6. adj.; v.; adj.
7. pron.; adv.; adv.; conj.
8. v.; adj.; adv.; adv.
9. adj.; n.; prep.; adj.; n.
10. adj.; adj.; adj.; adj.
11. pron.; prep.; adj.; n.; adv.; conj.
12. n.; pron.; adj.; adv.; adv.

B. 1. benches
2. flies
3. hero's or heroes'
4. pony's
5. watch's

C. The words in bold should be circled.

1. We plan to visit **Ottawa**, <u>the capital of Canada</u>, on our vacation.
2. My older **sister** <u>Kira</u> is an engineer.
3. We ate a hearty **breakfast**, <u>pancakes and ham</u>, before going to work.

Review (P. 81)

D. 1. gave   5. drive   9. doesn't   13. were
    2. rang   6. eaten   10. took   14. begun
    3. come   7. ran   11. did   15. fallen
    4. known   8. went   12. are   16. wasn't

E. 1. infinitive; to fish   4. infinitive; to finish
    2. gerund; Skating   5. participle; improved
    3. participle; flashing

F. The words in bold should be circled.

  1. he, **Mark**
  2. their, **workers**
  3. their, **Bob and Andre**
  4. her, **sister**
  5. them, **donations**

Using What You've Learned (P. 82)

B. Answers may vary. Possible answers include: which is a remote land in south-central Asia; Land of the Snows; Lhasa; who are sometimes called the hermit people; herders who roam about in the northern uplands of the country

C. 1. which; Tibet   3. who; herders
    2. who; Tibetans   4. that; things

D. Answers may vary. Possible answers include: in south-central Asia; of the World; of the Snows; in the world; of Tibet; of life; in the northern uplands; of the country; to the low regions; in tents; of yak hair; about the size; of a small ox; to the nomads; in the high altitudes

E. highest

F. Some

G. Answers may vary. Possible answers include: come; live; work

H. to see; to buy

I. Answers may vary. Possible answers include: or, and, because

Using What You've Learned (P. 83)

K. were

L. Answers may vary. Possible answers include: first, later, entirely, clearly, artistically, mechanically, Fortunately

M. Answers may vary. Possible answers include: was done, were used, was built, was made, is called

N. Answers may vary. Possible answers include: a system of writing based on pictures; a half-lion, half-man stone structure built for King Khafre

O. Answers may vary. Possible answers include: years, events, peace, system, reasons, culture, climate

P. Answers may vary. Possible answers include: people, Egyptians, Experts, writing, writings, pyramids, kings, hieroglyphics, pictures, steps, building, stone, monument, Great Sphinx, structure, King Khafre, Historians, buildings, materials, artifacts

Q. Answers may vary. Possible answers include: If, and, so

R. Answers may vary. Possible answers include: of years ago, around 3100 B.C., of their writing, on pyramids, for the kings, in them, in hieroglyphics, of writing, on pictures, for a number, of reasons, with hundreds, of steps, to the top, in the country, of stone, for King Khafre, about the ancient Egyptian people, in them, in Egypt

Unit 4   Capitalization and Punctuation

Lesson 65, Using Capital Letters (P. 84)

A. The first letter of the following words should be circled and capitalized:

  1. What
  2. Francis; The; Star; Spangled; Banner
  3. Edgar; The; Raven
  4. Paul; When
  5. Who; Snowbound; The; Barefoot; Boy
  6. What; Give

B. The first letter of the following words should be circled and capitalized:

  1. Miami; Florida; Atlanta; Georgia
  2. Potomac; River; Virginia; Maryland
  3. *Pinta; Niña; Santa Maria;* Columbus
  4. Spanish; Mississippi; River; English; Jamestown
  5. American; Red; Cross; Clara; Barton
  6. Rocky; Mountains; Andes; Mountains; Alps

Lesson 65, Using Capital Letters (P. 85)

C. The first letter of the following words should be circled and capitalized:

  1. Dr.; Thompson
  2. Mayor; Thomas
  3. Dr.; Crawford; W.; Long
  4. Mr.; Mrs.; Randall
  5. Senator; Dixon
  6. Gov.; Alden
  7. Ms.; Howell

D. The first letter of the following words should be circled and capitalized:

  1. Niles School Art Fair
    Sat., Feb. 8th, 9 A.M.
    110 N. Elm Dr.

  2. Shoreville Water Festival
    June 23–24
    Mirror Lake
    Shoreville, MN 55108

3. October Fest
October 28 and 29
9 A.M.–5 P.M.
63 Maple St.

4. Barbara Dumont
150 Telson Rd.
Markham, Ontario L3R 1E5

5. Captain C. J. Neil
c/o Ocean Star
P.O. Box 4455
Portsmouth, NH 03801

6. Dr. Charles B. Stevens
Elmwood Memorial Hospital
1411 First Street
Tucson, AZ 85062

Lesson 66, Using End Punctuation (P. 86)

A.
1. ?
2. .
3. ?
4. ?
5. .
6. .
7. ?
8. ?
9. .
10. .
11. ?
12. .
13. ?
14. ?

B. Did you know that experts say dogs have been around for thousands of years? In fact, they were the first animals to be made domestic. The ancestors of dogs were hunters. Wolves are related to domestic dogs. Like wolves, dogs are social animals and prefer to travel in groups. This is called pack behavior.

There have been many famous dogs throughout history. Can you name any of them? In the eleventh century, one dog, Saur, was named king of Norway. The actual king was angry because his people had removed him from the throne, so he decided to make them subjects of the dog. The first dog in space was a Russian dog named Laika. Laika was aboard for the 1957 journey of *Sputnik*. Most people have heard of Rin Tin Tin and Lassie. These dogs became famous in movies and television.

There are several hundred breeds of dogs throughout the world. The smallest is the Chihuahua. A Chihuahua weighs less than two pounds. Can you think of the largest? A Saint Bernard or a Mastiff can weigh over 150 pounds.

Lesson 67, Using Commas (P. 87)

A.
1. Frank, Mary, and Patricia are planning a surprise party for their parents.
2. It is their parents' fiftieth wedding anniversary, and the children want it to be special.
3. They have invited the people their father used to work with, their mother's garden club members, and long-time friends of the family.
4. Even though the children are grown and living in their own homes, it will be hard to make it a surprise.
5. Mr. and Mrs. Slaughter are active, friendly, and involved in many things.

6. For the surprise to work, everyone will have to be sure not to say anything about their plans for that day.
7. This will be especially hard for the Knudsens, but they will do their best.
8. Since every Sunday the families have dinner together, the Knudsens will have to become very good actors the week of the party.

B.
1. "We're sorry that we have to cancel our plans," said Earl.
2. Carmen said, "But we've done this every week for ten years!"
3. Jeannette said, "We have to leave town."
4. Ivan asked, "Can't you put it off just one day?"
5. "No, I'm afraid we can't," said Earl.
6. "Then we'll just start over the following week," said Carmen cheerfully.
7. Jeannette said, "I bet no one else has done this."
8. "I sure hate to spoil our record," said Earl.
9. "Don't worry about it," said Ivan.
10. "Yes, everything will work out," said Jeannette.

Lesson 67, Using Commas (P. 88)

C.
1. Dr. Perillo, a nutritionist, is an expert on proper eating.
2. "Students, it's important to eat a well-balanced diet," she said.
3. "Yes, but how do we know what the right foods are?" asked one student.
4. "First, you need to look carefully at your eating habits," said Dr. Perillo.
5. "Yes, you will keep a journal of the foods you eat," she said.
6. "Dr. Perillo, what do you mean by the right servings?" asked Emilio.
7. "Okay, good question," she said.
8. "A serving, Emilio, is a certain amount of a food," said Dr. Perillo.
9. "Dave, a cross-country runner, will need more calories than a less active student," explained Dr. Perillo.
10. "Class, remember to eat foods from the five basic food groups," she said.

D. Our neighbor, Patrick, has fruit trees on his property. "Patrick, what kinds of fruit do you grow?" I asked. "Well, I grow peaches, apricots, pears, and plums," he replied. "Wow! That's quite a variety," I said. Patrick's son, Jonathan, helps his dad care for the trees. "Oh, it's constant work and care," Jonathan said, "but the delicious results are worth the effort." After harvesting the fruit, Jonathan's mother, Allison, cans the fruit for use throughout the year. She makes preserves, and she gives them as gifts for special occasions. Allison sells some of her preserves to Chris Simon, the owner of a local shop. People come from all over the county to buy Allison's preserves.

Jonathan's aunt, Christina, grows corn, tomatoes, beans, and squash in her garden. Each year she selects her best vegetables and enters them in the fair. She has won blue ribbons, medals, and certificates for her vegetables. "Oh, I just like being outside. That's why I enjoy gardening," Christina said. Christina's specialty, squash-and-tomato bread, is one of the most delicious breads I have ever tasted.

Lesson 68, Using Quotation Marks and Apostrophes (P. 89)

A. 1. "Dan, did you ever play football?" asked Tim.
   2. Morris asked, "Why didn't you come in for an interview?"
   3. "I have never," said Laurie, "heard a story about a ghost."
   4. Selina said, "Yuri, thank you for the present."
   5. "When do we start on our trip to the mountains?" asked Stan.
   6. Our guest said, "You don't know how happy I am to be in your house."
   7. My sister said, "Kelly bought those beautiful baskets in Mexico."
   8. "I'm going to plant the spinach," said Doris, "as soon as I get home."

B. 1. players'   **4.** It's   **7.** Men's
   2. baby's   **5.** captain's
   3. isn't   **6.** doesn't

Lesson 69, Using Other Punctuation (P. 90)

A. 1. The play was going to be in an old-fashioned theater.
   2. The theater was so small that there were seats for only ninety-two people.
   3. The vice-president was played by Alan Lowe.

B. 1. At 2:10 this afternoon, the meeting will start.
   2. Please bring the following materials with you: pencils, paper, erasers, and a notebook.
   3. The meeting should be over by 4:30.
   4. Those of you on the special committee should bring the following items: cups, paper plates, forks, spoons, and napkins.

C. 1. Colleen is a clever teacher; she is also an inspiring one.
   2. Her lectures are interesting; they are full of information.
   3. She has a college degree in history; world history is her specialty.
   4. She begins her classes by answering questions; she ends them by asking questions.

Review (P. 91)

A. The letters that are capitalized should be circled, and end punctuation should be added as shown.
   1. Mr. J. C. Moran owns a car dealership in Chicago, Illinois.
   2. Jesse decided to apply for a job on Tuesday.
   3. Wow, Mr. Moran actually offered him a job!
   4. Jesse will start work in June.
   5. Jesse is the newest employee of Moran's Cars and Vans.
   6. Didn't he get auto experience when he lived in Minnesota?
   7. He also got training at Dunwoody Technical Institute.
   8. Jesse took some computer courses there taught by Mr. Ted Woods and Ms. Jane Hart.
   9. Jesse had only temporary jobs at Highland Cafe and Mayfield Electronics for the last two years.
   10. Since Jesse wants to be prepared for his new job, he checked out *Automobile Technology and the Automobile Industry* from the Windham Library.

B. 1. After Jesse got the new job, his family, friends, and neighbors gave him a party.
   2. Everyone brought food, drinks, and even some gifts.
   3. Bob, Jesse's roommate, and Carmen, Jesse's sister, bought him a briefcase.
   4. His mother and father bought him a new shirt, jacket, and tie for his first day on the job.
   5. His father congratulated him by saying, "Jesse, we are happy for you, and we wish you the best in your new job."
   6. Jesse replied, "Well, I'm also very excited about it, and I want to thank all of you for the party and the gifts."

C. 1. "How did you get so lucky, Jesse?" asked Mike.
   2. "It wasn't luck," answered Jesse, "because I studied before I applied for this job."
   3. "I didn't know you could study to apply for a job," said Mike, laughing.
   4. "Mike, I read an employment guide before I applied," said Jesse.
   5. "I have never heard of an employment guide!" exclaimed Mike.
   6. "It's a great book," said Jesse.
   7. "Jesse, I'd like to apply for a job at Moran's," said Mike.
   8. Jesse replied, "Why don't you read my guide to prepare for the interview?"

Review (P. 92)

D. 1. Joe King, Jesse's best friend, is the one who gave Jesse the employment guide to use for his interview at Moran's.

2. Jesse didn't know important interview skills.

3. The guide offered twenty-five helpful hints.

4. The guide suggested the following: dress neatly, be on time, be polite, and be enthusiastic.

5. Jesse also used the guide's suggestions for preparing a resume listing his work experience.

6. Jesse's list contained these items: his employers' names and addresses, dates of employment, and job descriptions.

7. The guide said Jesse should be a well-informed applicant, so he researched salespersons' duties and made a list of questions to ask.

8. Jesse's guide recommended getting to the interview early to have time to fill out the employer's application forms.

9. Jesse arrived at Mr. Moran's office at 3:45 for his 4:00 interview.

10. The interview lasted forty-five minutes, and Jesse was relaxed and self-confident when he left.

11. Mr. Moran's phone call the next day at 1:30 let Jesse know he had gotten the job.

12. Jesse needed to do the following: pick up a salesperson's manual, fill out employment forms, and enroll in the company's insurance program.

E.
73 E. River St.
Chicago, IL 65067
May 30, 2005

Dear Mr. Moran:

I just wanted to thank you for offering me the salesperson's position with your company. You mentioned in our interview that my duties would be the following: selling cars and vans, checking customers' credit references, and assisting customers with their paperwork. I've studied the automobile sales guide that you gave me, and I feel that I'm prepared to do a terrific job for Moran's. Thank you again. I'm looking forward to starting next Monday.

Sincerely,
Jesse Sanchez

Using What You've Learned (P. 93)

A. The letters that are capitalized should be circled.

Have you ever heard the story called "The Dog and His Bone"? There once was a dog that had a new bone. "This is a great bone," said the dog to himself. The dog decided to take a walk and carried the bone proudly in its mouth. He went down a dirt road and over a bridge. As he was crossing the bridge, he looked down into the river. "Wow!" said the dog. "Look at that big bone in the water!" The dog thought to himself, "I'd rather have that bone than the one I have right now." Can you guess what happened next? Well, the dog opened his mouth and dropped the bone—a foolish thing to do—into the river. When the splash of the bone hitting the water stopped, the dog looked for the bigger bone. However, he didn't see it anymore. What he did see was his old bone sinking to the bottom of the river.

There is an incredible man, Scott Targot, who lives in my town. His nickname is the Ironman. People call him Ironman Targot because he has won several triathlons. Do you know what a triathlon is? Some people consider it the ultimate sports contest. Athletes have to swim for 2.4 miles, ride a bike for 112 miles, and run for 26.2 miles. Just one of those alone is a lot of work. Scott will train from February to August in preparation for a triathlon in Hawaii. Scott says, "I wouldn't want to be doing anything else with my time." Each day during training, he gets up at 7:00, loosens up for a half-hour, then runs from 7:30 to 8:30. After he cools down a little, he takes a 20-mile bike ride. At the end of the ride, he swims for an hour and a half. "Yes, I get tired," he says, "but I usually feel refreshed after swimming." Last, he lifts light weights and takes a break to do some reading.

A triathlon is supposed to be completed in less than seventeen hours. The record is less than half that time. "That's my goal," says Scott. He's still trying to break 14 hours and ten minutes. Scott's usually one of the top finishers.

Using What You've Learned (P. 94)

B. Sir Walter Scott, one of the world's greatest storytellers, was born in Edinburgh, Scotland, on August 15, 1771. Walter had an illness just before he was two years old that left him lame for the rest of his life. His parents were worried, so they sent him to his grandparents' farm in Sandy Knowe. They thought the country air would do him good.

Walter's parents were right. He was quite healthy by the time he was six years old. He was happy, too. Walter loved listening to his grandfather tell stories about Scotland. The stories stirred his imagination. He began to read fairy tales, travel books, and history books. It was these early stories that laid the groundwork for Scott's later interest in writing stories. His most famous book, *Ivanhoe*, has been read by people around the world.

Check What You've Learned (P. 95)

A. 1. S   **3.** A
    2. H   **4.** H

B. jar

C. 1. S   **3.** P or S
    2. C   **4.** C

D. 1. I would
    2. do not

E. horrible

F. 1 should be circled.

G. The words in bold should be circled.

1. E; that, **is**
2. IM; (You), **read**
3. D; I, **am watching**
4. IN; Who, **wanted**

H. 1. CS
 2. CP

I. 1. CS
 2. I
 3. RO

J. Dana gave her the box of chocolates [that someone had sent].
            DO

Check What You've Learned (P. 96)

K. The words in bold should be circled.

Before **Edward** could stop his <u>car</u>, **Mr. Huang** opened the <u>door</u> and jumped out.

L. The words in bold should be circled.

Our local <u>newspaper</u>, ***The Hunterstown Gazette***, is the oldest in the state.

M. 1. past   3. future
 2. present   4. past

N. 1. began, ate   3. took, chose
 2. Teaching, been   4. set, laid

O. 1 should be circled.

P. The words in bold should be circled.
 1. SP; **We**   3. PP; **their**
 2. OP; **her**   4. IP; **Someone**

Q. The word in bold should be circled.

Annette served the wonderful dinner with <u>her</u> customary flair.

R. 1. adjective   4. adverb
 2. adverb   5. adjective
 3. adjective   6. adverb

S. The words in bold should be circled.

Hoan pretended to be asleep <u>when</u> his father came **into** <u>his room</u> to wake him **for** <u>breakfast</u>.

Check What You've Learned (P. 97)

T.

482 W. Franklin St.
Overhill, MT 80897
Aug. 22, 2005

Dear Ms. Muller:

I received the application you sent me, but these enclosures were not included: the aptitude test, the self-addressed envelope, and the postcard. Would you please send them as soon as possible? I want to complete everything just as you want it.

I'd like to confirm our appointment for Wednesday, September 14, at 3:15 P.M. I look forward to seeing you then and talking with you about the scholarship.

Yours truly,
Roy Thompson

Index